BEYOND THE BELL:

My Journey From Classroom to Corporate

By: **Calley Hood**

This book is very personal to me. It is my story of being in the classroom and the reasons I left. I realized teaching was not meant to be my forever career. If you picked up this book, maybe you are curious about leaving the classroom, too. If this grabbed your interest or attention, keep reading. I'm excited to share this journey with you.

MANY THANKS

Only a handful of people knew about this project, as I had to keep it under wraps because I was still teaching and didn't want anyone to know yet that I was going to leave my career. This book would not have been possible without the constant prayer and love from these wonderful people. Thank you to my mom, who knows me best, is always my sounding board, and my biggest source of comfort and support. Also, I am so appreciative to my friends and family, Carl, Traci, Jeanne, and Kim.

Another big thank you to my mentors, Leena and Erica, for their encouragement and for cheering me on during this huge transition in my life. They were always there for me if I needed to talk, text, or just needed to give them updates on my career search. And to Kathy, my career trainer, for her guidance and help along the way.

To my teachers and instructors, Ali, Alex, Erica, and others, for teaching me what I needed to know to thrive in my new career.

A big shout out to my team, WWID, and my cohorts who pushed me and helped me grow into my future career path. To the many people who answered questions and emails I sent to them. Thank you to those who reviewed sample work, gave feedback, and looked at my portfolio and resume.

A huge thank you to all of the many people in the social media groups I belong to. Your encouragement has been amazing! I have had so much reassurance from complete strangers that genuinely wanted to show support and offer inspiration.

And to these wonderful people for talking to me on the phone and video chats to help motivate and encourage me: Jill, Gretchen, Katie, Tim, and Heidi. I could not have done this without you. I am so grateful!

PREFACE

While this book is about why and how I left the classroom for greener pastures, I thought it was important to note that this project in no way takes away from the students I taught, connections I made, and the relationships I still have through my teaching career. I do not want this book to discount in any way some of the phenomenal parents I have met and the support they have shown me over the years. Even to this day, I am still friends and in contact with parents and students that I taught over a decade ago. Last year, I still exchanged Christmas gifts with former students, and right before Covid hit, past students were still helping get my classroom ready for the upcoming school year. I am grateful for the experiences I've had and the people I've met along the way. I am blessed to have worked with some wonderful co-teachers, paraprofessionals, and other staff and colleagues. Many of my friends are still teaching, and I am delighted to know that regardless of where my future takes me, I still get to call these folks my allies.

Even though I left teaching, I will forever be a lifelong learner and teacher — just in a different capacity.

To everything there is a season and a time to every purpose under Heaven

~Ecclesiastes 3:1

For me, being a classroom teacher was not meant to be a 30-year career. It was simply a season in my life, and that season is over.

WHAT THIS BOOK IS NOT

This book is in no way recruiting teachers to leave the profession. It is not a means of persuading teachers to get out of the education field or trying to get anyone to quit teaching. We need good educators, and I admire those who still have a love and passion for this career and those who will continue to influence and transform many lives.

WHAT THIS BOOK IS

To all the educators out there, I believe you deserve to be happy. Maybe at one time you were content, but now it seems you have lost that passion and spark. This book is a guide and a road map, a source of support and encouragement, for those who want to leave the classroom. It is a tool to use to look beyond the classroom for new growth and opportunity. This book was written for those who feel confined within classroom walls to show awareness that other prospects exist and there is a whole world out there with endless possibilities.

My Mission

Through my quest to leave the classroom, a revelation was revealed to me that I was not alone. There are A LOT of unhappy teachers also wanting to leave the education field, many of them in a similar boat as I was, not knowing where to turn. I realized that other people are going through what I was going through, and I knew that many more teachers were probably discontent in their careers but felt stuck. They don't know where to turn for help and support. Therefore, I felt there was a need for this book.

Throughout this entire process, I received so much help from not only friends and family, but also complete strangers as well. The amount of support was truly overwhelming. It came from people who went out of their way to encourage and promote me. Many of them had been in the education field themselves and knew what it was like before they made their transition. I also had help from others who were not in the education field, but simply had a soft spot in their heart for teachers. They spent so much of their time willing to share resources, their experiences, and situations they had gone through. Because of that, I hope I can pay it forward by helping others in the same way others helped me. Hopefully I will be able to mentor or inspire someone else. I made it my mission to return the favor. I hope this book helps struggling teachers as they find their way on a new journey, to a rewarding career, and finding happiness.

My Aspiration

Pursuing another career path is a very daunting and time-consuming task. I spent countless hours learning, exploring, and researching what I needed to do to find another job using the skills I already had along with the degrees I had acquired. My goal in writing this book is to save you precious time and energy by getting to the nitty-gritty of what you need to know, and actions you need to take to make a career switch in record time.

MY PURPOSE

This book was written for anyone who feels wedged in the classroom and wants to get out but doesn't know how. When I decided to leave, I didn't know where to go, what to do, or where to look. But through hours and hours of research, making connections, learning, and trial and error, I found my way. You do not have to do this alone. I have navigated and chartered these dark waters already, and I understand how you feel.

I hope this will be your road map that will guide you through the steps it will take to look beyond classroom walls and discover your new passion. I hope you will learn from my personal experiences and use this book as a resource.

Sometimes when you find yourself in a tough situation, it's encouraging to know that someone is rooting for you, and that someone who believes in you is in your corner. That being said, I'm cheering you on! I know where you are and what you are going through. I'm here to help you get through this. I hope my story gives you the courage you need to take your next steps.

GET YOUR GAME PLAN ON

You have to learn the rules of the game. And then you have to play better than anyone else.

~Albert Einstein

You must have a game plan. If you aim at nothing, you will hit it every time.

~Zig Ziglar

By the time you finish this book, I hope that you will have a game plan in place for getting yourself out of the classroom by following these steps:

1. Make your decision to leave and NEVER look back
2. Research job opportunities
3. Decide what you are going to do and how to get there
4. Learn as much as you can
5. Make connections
6. Update your resume to fit your new dream job
7. Apply
8. Get hired
9. Get out
10. Be happy

ON THE FENCE

Throw your heart over the fence and the rest will follow.

~Norman Vincent Peale

Don't sit on the fence too long…you are bound to get splinters.

~Michelle A. Homme

When you think of being "on the fence" about something, it is because you are undecided. It's almost like a seesaw where you are teetering back and forth trying to make up your mind. You see the benefits and disadvantages of both staying and leaving. But if you think back to when you were a kid playing on the playground, seesaws sometimes hurt. Sometimes the other person suddenly jumps ship and leaves you crashing to the ground.

If you are still on the fence about leaving the classroom, I suggest that you make a list of the pros and cons. What do you enjoy about your job? What do you like most about teaching? What do you like the least? What makes you stressed out? What is something you love about teaching that you would want to take with you to a new career? List your reasons to stay. List your reasons to go.

For example, a list of pros may be:
1. Working with kids
2. Summers off
3. Insurance

A list of cons may be:
1. Grading papers
2. Disengaged parents
3. Paperwork

I listed out all of the things I enjoyed about teaching. Then I listed out all of the things I disliked about it. In my case, the cons outweighed the pros.

Go ahead and make your lists of pros and cons. Get clear on what you like and don't like about teaching. Is this something you can see yourself still doing five years down the road? Would you be happier to find a new career path?

Beyond the Bell Bonus Tip:

Decide which side of the fence you fall on.

GET REAL ABOUT HOW YOU FEEL

Be who you are and say what you feel, because those who mind
don't matter and those who matter don't mind.

~Bernard M. Baruch

It's okay to show your vulnerability. There's power in that.

~Raquel Garcia

Y ou know yourself better than anyone else. Listen to your gut and how you feel. You don't need to explain yourself to anyone. Ask yourself, how does this job make me feel? How long have I felt this way? Then write down your honest answers.

When I first began my teaching career, this is how I felt.

How I felt at school:

⊙   Excited, thankful, like I was making a difference

How administration made me feel:

⊙   Supported, welcome, appreciated

How my classroom made me feel:

⊙   Creative, inspired, loved

As my teaching career went on, my feelings began to change. When I created my list of pros and cons and I discovered that my cons list was longer than my pros list, I knew there was a problem. Into my last year of teaching, I did this exercise, and this is an example of what I wrote.

How I felt at school:

⊙   Trapped, anxious, stuck, defeated, apprehensive, overwhelmed, overworked

How administration made me feel:

- Inadequate, bullied, substandard, picked on, singled out, frustrated, resentful, demoralized

How my classroom made me feel:

- Stressed out, anxious, guarded, fatigued

Write out your "get real statements." Mine were:

- I am unhappy.
- I am not going to continue working at this job another year.
- I deserve better.

I did not want to feel this way anymore, especially at a job in which I spent a third of my day. I don't want you to feel this way either.

What about you? How do you feel? How would you fill in these blanks?

I am _____

I am not _____

I deserve _____

Your feelings are not something you can just sweep under the rug. Now that you are being honest with how you feel, what are you going to do about it?

Beyond the Bell Bonus Tip:
Be brutally honest about how you feel.

GET RID OF THE GUILT

Move forward with no second-guessing, no guilt trips, no hesitation. Your purpose is to recreate yourself anew in each moment.

~Neale Donald Walsch

Remove anger, regret, worry, resentment, guilt, and blame. Then watch your health and life improve.

~Charles F. Glassman

I think a lot of teachers who consider leaving the classroom experience a sense of guilt. Guilt because they are leaving a career they felt committed to. They experience guilt because they feel like they are quitting. They feel they are giving up on their school and co-workers. They are guilty for leaving students who need them. They feel guilty because they made a commitment for 30 years, but they are cutting that short. They feel guilty for spending so much time going to college for student teaching, teaching degrees, advanced degrees, and endorsements. They feel guilty for spending thousands of dollars on student loans for a career they no longer want.

I felt this way too. I thought teaching would be my only career. I felt a sense of guilt because I have what a lot of people would want in their professional lives—a career, years of experience, and advanced degrees. I was already past the halfway mark to retirement. I only had 12 more years to go. I was raised from a very young age to finish what I start. In a way, I felt like I wasn't following through with what I was brought up to do. I've had several family members make comments to me like, "You've got a great job! You're so fortunate." Maybe so, but they weren't living my life and going through the day-to-day with me. None of that mattered because I wasn't happy. I felt guilty because I wanted to leave.

I discovered that the average person will change careers five to seven times during their working life according to career change statistics. It is also important to point out that over 40% of teachers leave the profession within five years of starting. Why should I (and you) feel guilty for leaving and changing careers?

So, what am I saying to you? I'm saying that you should not feel guilty for leaving. It's okay to leave. And it's okay to be happy. You have not wasted years, education, or experience. You can still use the skills you learned in college and in the classroom and apply them to a new career.

Beyond the Bell Bonus Tip:

Instead of feeling guilty for wanting to leave, think about how unfair it would be to you and your students if you stayed in a career that your heart's not in anymore.

MAKE YOUR DECISION

Be decisive. Make a decision. The road of life is paved with flat squirrels who couldn't make a decision.

~Unknown

The first step towards getting somewhere is to decide that you are not going to stay where you are.

~J.P. Morgan

You are being presented with two choices: Evolve or Repeat.

~Unknown

I know making a decision can be difficult. This is especially true when you are talking about your career. For many of us, being a classroom teacher felt like a safe career because there will always be a need for teachers. It means a steady income and receiving a paycheck each month. It means you also have benefits including health, dental, life insurance, and retirement. If you've been in the education field for a while, it is also considered your comfort zone, which makes it even more difficult to leave; therefore, leaving teachers feeling stuck in the profession.

I feel that many teachers get locked into this career and feel like they can't leave because they don't know what else to do. They do not know that another career path exists. So they keep "hanging on." They think that maybe things will get better. Or they may say to themselves, "It's not that bad," they then end up being stuck another year. That turns into another 10 years. This is what happened to me. I might have had a really bad day or a few bad days and would leave work completely exhausted and in tears wanting to quit. But then I would have a good week or two, and think to myself, "Oh, it's not as bad as I think," and then I'd end up staying another year. This pattern repeated over and over again. I was 18 years into the profession and still feeling this way. There is no one to blame but myself for not leaving sooner.

I knew I had to make a decision. I knew if I stayed another year, it would completely crush my spirit. I finally got the courage and strength to demand better for myself. As soon as I made up my mind, I got to work on figuring out a new future and what was going to make me happy. I had to depend on myself to make changes. I made this decision myself and for my self-worth. I had to do this for my health, happiness, and future.

If this sounds like you, you need to take action. Make a choice. If you decide to stay, it is your choice. If you decide to leave, it is also your choice. Whatever you're not changing, you are choosing. But you have got to be okay with whichever choice you choose.

Once you have made your decision, stick with it. Be fully committed. This is not a transition and life change you can partially be in. You are either all in or not at all.

Ask yourself, what direction is my future? And then how would you finish this sentence: If I continue down this path ...

Beyond the Bell Bonus Tip:
Make a decision that will make you happy, not full of regret.

YOU ARE NOT ALONE

You are not alone in the struggle of life. Entire cosmos is with you. It evolves through the way you face and overcome challenges of life. Use everything in your advantage.

~Amit Ray

Empathy is a strange and powerful thing. There is no script. There is no right way or wrong way to do it. It's simply listening, holding space, withholding judgment, emotionally connecting, and communicating that incredibly healing message of "You're not alone."

~Brene Brown

At the beginning of this process, I felt very alone, especially at work. I felt isolated. I felt this for a lot of reasons. Mainly because I wanted to leave, but I had hardly ever heard of anyone leaving the teaching profession early. They all seemed to stay till retirement, and some even beyond their 30 years. And some teachers even returned after they retired! Sure, I heard a lot of teachers talk about leaving. I heard them say they were going to quit or retire early, but that was just talk. It was rare if a teacher actually did. Why? I think for a lot of them it was because they felt stuck and didn't know what else they could do with a teaching degree.

One of the biggest takeaways while going through this transition was that I found out I was not alone. I discovered there are many unhappy teachers wanting to get out of this profession. I also learned that most of them also feel like they are alone.

If anyone reading this feels the same way, I want to reassure you, you are not alone. You are not alone in wanting to get out of teaching. You are not alone in the process of finding a new career. You are not alone in feeling conflicted about your decision. And you do not have to figure out what to do next alone either.

Beyond the Bell Bonus Tip:

Connect with others who are going through a similar experience.

YOU'RE NOT STUCK

You're Not Stuck. You're just committed to certain patterns of behavior because they helped you in the past. Now those behaviors have become more harmful than helpful. The reason why you can't move forward is because you keep applying an old formula to a new level in your life. Change the formula to get a different result.

~Emily Maroutian

You are not stuck where you are unless you decide to be.

~Wayne W. Dyer

It is when you are going through the most difficult chapter in life that your hero is revealed, and how beautiful it is when you finally realize—You have the strength to save yourself.

~Dodinsky

When I hear the word "stuck," I'm reminded of a hike I took years ago with a friend of mine. We had been on many hikes together with our dogs, and I enjoyed her friendship and company. We always avoided crowds and took the road less traveled. One day she called me and asked if I wanted to meet her for a hike, and of course I agreed. Hiking was and still is one of my favorite ways to spend time outdoors. At the beginning of the trailhead, she mentioned that this hike should be around five or six miles. We began our adventure and admired the beautiful scenery. I was enjoying all the fresh mountain air, knowing our hike was soon about to come to an end ... or so I thought. Well, at about the six-mile mark, we were nowhere close to being finished. There was no one around, no cars, no trail signs, nothing. We were on top of the mountain, in the woods, tired and hungry. I felt stuck on the trail and thought I was never going to get finished. And it wasn't because I didn't love hiking. It was because I had mentally prepared myself before we began that we were going to hike five or six miles, not 12 miles (which is what we actually walked)! It was mind over matter. We kept trudging along, and stopped for breaks along the way. I had no other choice but to keep going. I knew we wouldn't be on the trail forever, even though it felt like it at the time.

In the same way, being "stuck" stirs up emotions of how I felt in the classroom. I felt like I was fastened and frozen and couldn't find my way out. It's terrible that our jobs make us feel this way sometimes. You keep wanting to escape, but you can't move, and your attempts to make it better only make it worse. Every attempt seems to be counterproductive. But the good news is, you are not stuck. You got yourself into this situation, and you can get yourself out.

I remember recently telling my mom that teaching in my school system reminded me of John Grisham's book *The Firm*. It made me feel like I was trapped and couldn't go anywhere. And because I was "vested," they could do whatever they wanted with me because I live in a small town without many other options for someone with a teaching degree, so "the firm" had control of me, and I felt trapped. It was a terrible feeling.

At this very moment, it may seem like you are stuck. You feel attached to your career. You want to let go, but it keeps pulling you back and forth like a game of tug-of-war. You may feel at a standstill, like you are left stationary by some sort of obstruction. You feel hindered and permanently affixed. You may feel completely boxed in and can't go anywhere. You feel trapped. You know you want to take action, but you feel paralyzed from the neck down, leaving you unable to move forward or make a decision. Believe me, I've been where you are and have felt what you are feeling.

No matter how you feel right now, you are not stuck, and you can get out of this situation. As bad as it may feel and seem right now, you are simply in need of a change. Once you can admit that, then start taking baby steps toward a new situation so you do not feel wedged in a place where you are unhappy.

Think about the tools you have and the resources available to you. Try using what you already have to pry your way out. Maybe you can get one foot out, then push out your second foot. Soon you will be all the way out of your sticky mess.

Most of feeling stuck comes from our mindset. This comes from not knowing what is out there in terms of other career choices and options, and you feel like you can't do anything else. Once we change our mindset, we have a world of opportunities at our disposal. Believing in ourselves is like seeing a small slit of light from the cracks and crevices of a dark wooden floor where we can see that something else is out there.

There is more to life than teaching. There is also life after teaching. Life does not end when you leave the classroom. There are plenty of careers and opportunities out there for you to explore. The education and degrees you have earned do not limit you. They do not define you and what you can do.

Start taking steps, however small, toward your goal. This will unhinge you so you don't feel stagnant, and you will be able to move forward, and in no time at all, you will start seeing some much-needed change.

Beyond the Bell Bonus Tip:

Remember, you are not stuck. This is simply mind over matter.

Change Is Scary

Making a big life change is pretty scary. But know what's even scarier? Regret.

~Zig Ziglar

When it feels scary to jump, that's exactly when you jump. Otherwise you end up staying in the same place your whole life. And that I can't do.

~Abel Morales

Always go with the choice that scares you the most, because that is the one that is going to help you grow.

~Caroline Myss

Don't let the concept of change scare you as much as the concept of staying unhappy.

~Timber Hawkeye

A lot of people struggle with change. Change is hard. I think it is so difficult to make a change within ourselves or make a change in what we do or how we have been doing something because it requires us to evolve. People are creatures of habit and in order to change, we have to step out of our comfort zone. And for many people the feeling is so uncomfortable that they avoid it at all costs because it is stepping into the unknown. It is easier to stay in a place or situation where we feel hopeless, frustrated or unsatisfied than it is to make a change.

Think about dieting. A lot of people want to lose weight. It is the number one goal for New Year's resolutions. Most people know they should be drinking more water, exercising at least five times a week, avoiding sugar, and lowering carb intake. It's not that they don't know how to diet, it's actually making the change that is so difficult because it's uncomfortable. And they have to discipline themselves for a while before seeing the difference the change has made. Changing a career is no different in that regard. It's usually a bigger step than dieting, even though they both deal with our well-being.

For me, this was a scary change. It was walking into the unknown. It was so different from what I had done for the past 18 years. I had fear of failure and judgment. I was filled with confusion and anxiety. I mean, this job was part of my identity. I knew I was letting go of a lot of security. At my current job, I had insurance, a steady paycheck, holiday breaks, summers and weekends off. I was giving all of that up. And because I'm single, I knew I didn't have another income to fall back on if something were to happen and the job didn't work out as I hoped.

But I knew it was something I had to do. I was not happy, and I knew I needed a change. I left my safety net and comfort zone and took a gamble at a new career for the sake of my health and happiness. I knew if I could get over this hurdle of fear of the unknown, I would be the happiest I had ever been and would wonder why I hadn't left years ago.

Beyond the Bell Bonus Tip:
Don't let fear be the reason you stay!

TAKE A RISK

You sometimes lose by taking risks, but you always lose by holding back.

~Rachel Wolchin

Take risks. If you win, you will be happy. If you lose, you will be wise.

~Unknown

And the day came when the risk to remain tight in a bud was greater than the risk it took to bloom.

~Anais Nin

We typically approach risk reluctantly. Why? Because of fear of the unknown. It is more comfortable to play it safe than to take a gamble on uncertainty.

Taking a risk requires courage. No matter the outcome, we still win. If we achieve our goal, we win. If we don't achieve our goal, we still win because we gained experience and learned from it.

Most of us are familiar with the quote, "the greater the risk, the greater the reward," but what does that really mean? It is essentially saying the greater the risk, the higher the potential reward. And what does this mean regarding your career and current situation? It means you need to calculate your risk and see if the trade-off will be worth it.

What do you have to lose? If you are still reading this book, that tells me you're still considering a career move. You're not happy where you are, and the idea of leaving your current job for something possibly better is a risk you are willing to take.

Start working on your goal. Start somewhere, but you have to begin. Come to terms with the idea that you may fail, but you could also achieve something amazing.

Do it for yourself. That is your reason. And you are worth it.

Take action consistently. Any progress—whether it is great or small.

Get out of your comfort zone but take a risk with caution and not blindly.

Steps to taking a risk:

1. Learn and gather as much information as you can
2. Assess the pros and cons
3. Learn

Benefits of taking risks:

1. Limitless opportunity
2. Courage—because it helps us build belief in ourselves

Retrain your mind. Instead of thinking of risk as negative, think of it as an opportunity to succeed. Taking risks shows confidence and shows you are not a follower. You are a leader. Both of which most employers look for when hiring.

Beyond the Bell Bonus Tip:

Take the leap! You'll never know what awaits or what doors could open.

MY STORY

This is my life ... my story ... my book. I will no longer let anyone else write it; Nor will I apologize for the edits I make.

~Steve Maraboli

One day you will tell your story of how you overcame what you went through and it will be someone else's survival guide.

~Brene Brown

School, education, and learning have always been a part of my life. I grew up in a long line of teachers from both sides of my family. I guess you could say I kind of fell into this career path. I don't really believe I had a "calling" for it like some people have with their careers. I never woke up one day and said that teaching was what I'm supposed to do. However, I knew I loved kids and I also knew I could explain concepts in ways others could understand. I believe that a lot of my direction came from the small town where I grew up and knowing there were not a lot of job opportunities.

Growing up, I enjoyed school. As a little girl, I remember coming home from school and after a quick snack, I would go to my room and retrieve old, discarded textbooks about various subjects and play school. I was the teacher, usually with the same name as my current teacher, and occasionally my stuffed animals would turn into my students. And sometimes they even had the same names as students in my class. It was funny how those teddy bears, with the same names of classmates, kept getting into trouble. I would do this for hours. Mom would call down the hall that dinner was ready, so I would go eat and leave my "class" to finish their math page so we could check it together when I returned. I practiced "wait time" and would find myself mimicking my current or former teachers in what they said or did. I even retaught lessons that my "pupils" didn't understand.

During high school, we had to choose our career paths, either college or tech prep. I actually chose both and got a dual seal but started my college journey a week or two after graduating high school at a local private college for their summer semester. I remember crying on my first day. The workload was not what I was used to, and I felt like I didn't really get a break between finishing my senior year and before beginning college. But I pressed on and ended up graduating with an associate's degree a couple of years later.

Then I enrolled in another private college about an hour from my house. I ended up living on campus for about a year and commuting the rest of the time. Right before my student teaching semester and earning my bachelor's degree, I began taking some classes for my master's degree. I had already been approved for their master's program, and they allowed me to take up to two courses over the summer before finishing my four-year degree. In the fall of the same year, I completed my third grade student teaching semester and received my bachelor's degree.

The following summer, I was hired and took my first teaching job as a pre-K teacher. It wasn't my first choice, but I knew it was a foot in the door, so I took what I could get, and I was excited to begin!

I only taught pre-K for one year, and before that year was finished, I got a phone call from the elementary school principal for an interview. I got the job and began teaching fifth grade the following year. That year, I also finished my master's degree.

Shortly after that, I applied to another private university for my Educational Specialist degree. I was accepted and started that summer. It was great because it was a yearlong program that met once a month, and twice a month in the summer, and it was through a cohort at a college about an hour and a half from my house. The workload wasn't too bad, and most of it was done in groups.

I felt so great having accomplished as much as I had in a relatively short amount of time. I was at the beginning of my teaching career with endless possibilities ... or so I thought. Once I got started in the classroom, I realized that it is not what I signed up for.

Beyond the Bell Bonus Tip:

Don't be afraid that you might have a different ending to your story than you had in mind.

I Didn't Sign Up for This

If opportunity doesn't knock, build a door.

~Milton Berle

If you feel "burnout" setting in, if you feel demoralized and exhausted, it is best, for the sake of everyone, to withdraw and restore yourself.

~Dalai Lama

You don't have to spend the rest of your life feeling miserable at work, because there is a path to work that matters—to work that is fulfilling and created just for you.

~Ken Coleman

I was so excited! I finished college! I received my degree! I earned my teaching certification! I got hired! I was officially an employed teacher, something I had worked so hard for the past four years.

I was ecstatic. This was the start of my first "real" job and the beginning of my career. My dreams were finally coming true. I couldn't wait to go spend a fortune on cutesy accessories and decorate my very own classroom. I would soon be able to teach my first group of students.

Bruises and scrapes and the occasional loose tooth I expected, but I didn't sign up to be in the medical realm and sit by the classroom door with a face mask on taking temperatures every day, handle fatal food allergies, students with asthma, check for head lice, learn CPR, and sanitize the room each day. I didn't feel comfortable administering Epi-pens, especially when a student's life could possibly depend on it.

I didn't sign up to be in the legal sector either. I didn't sign up to somehow get pulled by both sides of a custody battle and get subpoenaed by both parents to go to court on the first day of my Christmas vacation.

The parents thought I would have something to say to make the judge sway in their favor based on my observations. I didn't sign up for having to contact my own attorney on multiple occasions because I felt I was being treated unfairly or because I questioned certain situations at my workplace.

I didn't sign up for bureaucracy. Bureaucracy and red tape have caused teachers to lose their freedom and respect. What I quickly realized was teaching wasn't all I thought it would be. There are so many constraints. Teachers can't teach what they want or when they want. Rules have regulations, and regulations have rules. When anything negative happens at school, it seems the teacher is usually blamed. It is irrelevant that teachers have years of education on how to teach, yet they are judged and rated by people who have little to no classroom experience. As teachers, we are supposed to accept whatever is said to us with no rebuttal.

I didn't sign up for this. I didn't sign up for all the other responsibilities that are expected of teachers. I didn't sign up to wear so many different hats. I signed up to make a difference and change lives. You know, fill the gaps. But I soon found out that college did not prepare me for this path because I didn't sign up for this.

Beyond the Bell Bonus Tip:

It's okay to leave a situation you did not sign up for.

23

TEACHERS DON'T TEACH

*Teaching seems to require the sort of skills one would need to
pilot a bus full of live chickens backwards, with no brakes, down
a rocky road through the Andes while providing colorful and
informative commentary on the scenery.*

~Franklin Habit

One of the reasons I got into education was to make a difference and
to change lives. I got into education to teach. I enjoy watching kids
learn. You know that amazing moment when your students finally get
that "Aha" light bulb moment and everything just suddenly clicks.
Sounds like an amazing career, right? Seeing all of that learning and
discovery happen before your own eyes. But what I quickly realized was
that teachers don't teach.

What?! Did I really say that? Yes, so just hear me out. Okay, so
teachers teach occasionally, but usually end up having to teach to a test
because of all the pressure for high test scores. With all of the "extras"
that are put on teachers' plates, teaching falls by the wayside.

Many people think that teachers have it made. I've heard so many
people say things like: You work Monday through Friday. You have
weekends off. You have the whole summer off. You get every holiday
off. While these statements are true, these statements are usually made by
people who do not have a clue about what teachers are required to do on
a daily basis.

**Here is just a small snapshot of job titles from a typical day in the life of
a teacher:**

- ⊙ Door greeter
- ⊙ Attendance taker
- ⊙ Administrator of transportation changes

- ⊙ Breakfast counter
- ⊙ Lunch counter
- ⊙ Test proctor
- ⊙ Note collector
- ⊙ Paper distributor
- ⊙ Recess monitor
- ⊙ Bathroom supervisor
- ⊙ Lesson planner
- ⊙ Severe weather drill instructor
- ⊙ Fire drill instructor
- ⊙ Lockdown drill instructor
- ⊙ Money collector
- ⊙ Epi-pen nurse
- ⊙ Shoulder to cry on
- ⊙ Moderator
- ⊙ Band-aid distributor
- ⊙ Desk cleaner
- ⊙ Certified CPR administrator
- ⊙ Nurse pass distributor
- ⊙ Data interpreter

And yet more duties and responsibilities expected of a teacher:

- ⊙ Parent conferences
- ⊙ Get supplies for students who do not have them
- ⊙ Provide coats in the winter
- ⊙ Check for lice
- ⊙ Replace shoes when there are holes in them or flip-flops break
- ⊙ Walk kids to the correct bus
- ⊙ Keep a grade book
- ⊙ Collect cellphones that ring during class
- ⊙ Replace earbuds
- ⊙ Charge Chromebooks
- ⊙ Get families help during the holidays
- ⊙ Report suspected neglect
- ⊙ Schedule guest speakers

- Monitor websites students get on to make sure they are appropriate
- Report suspected child abuse
- Paperwork
- Mandate reporting
- Compliance director training
- Professional development
- Certification requirements
- Data entry
- Text parents
- Create newsletters
- Return phone calls
- Implement rewards
- Grade papers
- Grade level meetings
- Faculty meetings
- Deal with disengaged parents
- Make sure students walk quietly down the hall and in a straight line
- Make copies
- Schedule outreach programs
- Organize field trips
- Fix signed paper folders
- Filing
- Review student records
- Enter grades
- Work at fundraiser festivals
- Parent nights

And then when Covid hit, the duties just piled on top of that. I was now also responsible for:

- Taking temperatures every day
- Releasing students to classrooms earlier
- Measuring distance between desks
- Social distancing in classrooms, hallways, and bathrooms

- Breakfast in the classroom every day
- Lunch in the classroom every other day
- Mandated face masks on at all time except when eating or drinking
- Sanitizing desks
- Multiple seating charts
- Transporting books and materials from school to home for virtual days
- Managing online and face-to-face students all at the same time

And did you notice something? None of those things I mentioned had anything to do with actual teaching!

For a long time, I thought it was just me. I thought I was doing or feeling something wrong. Shouldn't I be happy with this job? The other "stuff" outweighed all the positives. My heart wasn't in it anymore because teachers don't teach.

Beyond the Bell Bonus Tip:

Give yourself credit for all of the "extras" you do outside of your job description.

THIS JOB CHANGED ME

A toxic work environment is more likely to change you than you are to change it.
Get out.

~Octavia Butler

There are three solutions to every problem: accept it, change it or leave it. If you can't accept it, change it. If you can't change it, leave it.

~Unknown

Each year I've been in the classroom has changed me. And not all of those years were full of positive changes. Every year I felt myself slipping a little more away from who I was. I lost myself in this job. I wasn't *me* anymore.

I wasn't smiling. I wasn't laughing. I wasn't happy. I lost most of my creativity. I was irritable all the time. I had low self-esteem due to feeling devalued. My quality of life had been depleted.

I lost sight of who I was. My life was out of balance. I wasn't myself and I was sleeping my life away, which my doctor informed me was a sign of depression. I had anxiety. I felt drained. This job literally sucked the life out of me.

When school would start back in the fall, I wouldn't talk to anyone, family or friends, for about a week or two until I could get myself back into a schedule and my body adjusted. I was irritable, frustrated, and miserable. I lost my passions for things I normally loved. I didn't want to listen to music. I remember driving to and from school many days with just silence in the car. With so much going on, I was easily irritated at the end of the day. I didn't want to be around kids. I wanted to have silence.

Or sometimes I simply craved an adult conversation. I didn't want to read books. I stopped caring about things that were once important to me.

I felt like I was aging. I felt like years were slipping away from my life. I had gained weight, and my face stayed broken out due to stress. I felt so unhealthy.

I was always tired. I was sleeping. All. The. Time. And because I was sleeping every chance I could get, I couldn't sleep at night, even with sleeping pills.

I found myself crying a lot. I remember driving to meet some friends for dinner. I cried on the way there, I burst into tears at the dinner table, and I cried again in the car on the way home.

I felt like I was going into battle each day, therefore, I would spend the weekend resting and licking my wounds before beginning a new week. And then I would get the Sunday night blues, dreading going into work Monday morning.

I spent my summers trying to recoup and get ready for the next year. I was always looking for the weekend, the next holiday, the next break, or for summer. I wasn't happy. I wasn't myself. I was in constant survival mode and wishing my life away.

Beyond the Bell Bonus Tip:

If your job is changing who you are in a negative way, it's time to get out!

The Double Standard

In the end, leadership comes down to consistency and strong, confident action upon which the team can rely—and this doesn't mean imposing a bunch of rules.

~Don Yaeger

A narcissist lives by a certain set of rules otherwise known as "double standards." You will be expected to abide by these rules. However these exact same rules won't apply to them!

~Anne McCrea

Double standards are all around us. They are literally everywhere we look. They are essentially rules that are unfairly applied to different people or groups. It's the application of different sets of principles for situations. Certain people are basically given more latitude than others. Double standards are unfair. Unfortunately, double standards are everywhere, including in all facets in the school setting.

Teachers are expected to always respond in a timely and courteous manner to parents. But why is it okay for parents to not respond to notes or emails that teachers send regarding their child? Or even ignore texts from teachers? But if teachers don't respond, then we would be written up. Why is it okay for parents to not show up for conferences? It's okay for parents to say bad things about teachers behind their backs, bully them, or write nasty notes to them, and we are expected to smile and be courteous and professional.

Teachers are expected to put others and their children as our top priority. Most of the time this is other parents' kids and not our own.

Principals talk about how communication is so important, but when a teacher receives concerning feedback about their performance and gives memorandums to their principal asking to discuss it, and they don't respond for months, how is that okay? I remember one principal I had who caught wind of a bunch of teachers going to a board of education meeting. This principal called a hall meeting and told us to "behave" at the meeting. I'm guessing because she thought we might embarrass her? I also recall where I had some behavior students and therefore had "folders" to fill out each segment of every day. I wrote what I observed during the day and was very thorough and even took notes on what I witnessed, but because I wrote what I observed and not what the principal wanted me to write, I got into trouble.

There is also a lot of favoritism among other staff. One teacher may do something that administrators are okay with, while another teacher does the same thing and gets into trouble. It just depends on who you are, how much of a brown-noser you are, and how well you are going to make the admin or school look. I remember being in a meeting and a teacher made a comment in front of the principal asking if we could keep parents from coming into the school for parties and activities even after Covid was over. If I had said that, I would have gotten into trouble, but because of who said it, it was considered funny. Another teacher called a student an "idiot," but the admin laughed and told her not to do it again. If I had done that, I would have been fired. It's all in who you are.

There is inequity among teachers. For some behavior and pull-out teachers, they have been able to just not have kids that day and do whatever they need to do while the regular ed teachers have kids all day and barely get a break. The others just sit in their room and don't offer to help with anything. Or some teachers get to take a partial or full professional day or get to work on data, IEPs, and reports, but regular ed teachers do not.

Teachers have no work-life balance. We are expected to sacrifice additional countless hours and energy off contract "for the kids," and the only response we get is, "that is why you have supplemental pay."

If your school is anything like mine, admin move faculty and staff all around the building and to different schools, when most principals have no idea what it is like to have to pack up and set up a classroom. They act as if it is no big deal. Teacher evaluations do not reflect anything regarding student attendance or support they receive or lack thereof at home. Teachers are told to greet students and parents, but administrators do not do it themselves. Our teacher observations are based on differentiating instruction for all the different learners, yet students have to take standardized tests. Teachers are told to give feedback to students and to also implement in parent conferences and conversations the sandwich method, where you put a criticism in between two compliments. But how often do administrators do that with teachers? Admin like to lower expectations for students and parents while raising them for teachers. The powers that be also like to require everyone to receive training on something that is the fault of only a few because they never target just the problem teacher. They like to encourage us to collaborate, but then tell us what to do. Administrators claim they value critical thinking and encourage us to instill that within our students, but do not want teachers to question anything, have an opinion, or think outside the box. And if we do, we are considered going against authority. They constantly tell us, "You can handle it," when we have extra duties that need to be filled or more paperwork or training to attend, yet we are never treated like professionals. They also ask us to prioritize our relationships with students, but never form one with us.

The central office mandates training. Professional development is one-size-fits-all, whether you have 30 years or three years. This would not be acceptable in our classrooms, so why is it acceptable among staff? Professional development is mainly just talk and showing you what it would look like in a model world, but not realistic and not modeling what we can actually do in our classrooms with time and financial constraints. Districts are quick to tell everyone to learn a new program and teach with fidelity and rigor but change it just as soon as we learn well enough for it to start working. They never stick with anything long enough to see the results come to fruition. So much time and money are lost in trainings, meetings, planning, implementing, only to be discarded because something new is coming.

Schools say that we should do whatever is best for the students, no matter how it impacts the teacher. There is no regard for the teacher and how we feel. This negative impact, no matter how hard we try, will have a ripple effect for the students and the rest of the class. They want multiple new programs implemented at once. They often state there is no extra money for things that would be beneficial for the school, classroom, or students, but then realize that someone at the central office got a raise, or a new position just miraculously opened up for the new football coach's wife.

The hypocrisy is everywhere! Staff are overworked and stressed out trying to cope. Why can't we treat others equally, and be treated in the same way?

Beyond the Bell Bonus Tip:

Try to find a place where double standards have less of an impact on your professional life.

MY ESCALATING SNOWBALL

*I compare it with a lie, which like a snowball, the longer it is
rolled the greater it becomes.*

~Martin Luther

*The older I get, the greater power I seem to have to help the
world; I am like a snowball—the further I am rolled the more I
gain.*

~Susan B. Anthony

If you are praying for a blizzard, please go to Dairy Queen.

~Unknown

Most people usually think of a snowball effect as a positive action. Something that starts out small and gradually grows bigger and bigger as it picks up momentum. So, when the snowball has reached a substantial size, it keeps rolling and the momentum is almost unstoppable.

However, my snowball was growing in a negative way. Wanting and needing to leave the classroom came from years and years of buildup from stress, anxiety, and unhappiness. It wasn't something that happened over night. But it kept growing negative momentum at an uncontrollable rate.

As if regular and normal days of teaching aren't hard enough already, here are a few of my upsetting experiences that led to my growing snowball.

Some of the stress came from students. Over the years, I've had students who were violent, and I had to evacuate the classroom on multiple occasions because I didn't know if they would hurt another student or hurt me. I had one student who crawled on the floor and wrapped himself around the Christmas tree and refused to get up. I've had students who've thrown chairs and books and pushed over desks.

Teaching also brings sadness. One year I had a student who passed away from a brain tumor. To this day, I still have the flowers he gave me on the Friday before he passed away. I also remember having a student who was so poor that she asked me if her mom could clean my house for money. It ripped my heart in two.

Other stresses came from parents. Years ago, a group of malicious parents ganged up on me and tried to find fault in everything that I did. They thought they were better than everyone else simply because of the family they came from within the county. They felt that their children could do no wrong and there was no way they could make less than an "A" on everything.

I had another parent make false complaints about me at the board of education, which was later revoked. I've also had countless parents that were just rude or disengaged or didn't care about their child's education and future.

Other anxiety came from the staff that I worked with. Some talked about me behind my back. Or some discussed my teaching skills, style, and management, but had no idea how I taught because they had never observed me. I had one colleague who got onto me because I didn't give up my lunch break to go meet with a parent who just decided to show up with no scheduled conference. She made me feel guilty for not dropping everything to go meet with them. I also had a married colleague develop feelings for me, and his wife contacted me on several occasions because she thought something was going on between us.

Some of my unhappiness came from administration. I have worked under a number of admin over the years, some I enjoyed more than others. One of my admins had a side business and asked me to forge my sister's signature on a legal document. She actually called me out of class up to her office to see if I would sign my sister's name. One of them was extremely manipulative. She did anything she could think of to get her staff to do what she wanted. And she twisted your words around into getting you to do what she needed you to do instead of coming out and asking you. And I will never forget her telling me that "I cared too much." Another admin called me into her office and asked if I "liked my job." I also had an administrator basically stalk me on a dating website. I mean, I could understand clicking on my profile and then realizing who it was and not view the profile again, but no, this administrator kept viewing my profile over and over again. And each time he did, I was notified of it. How creepy is that?! On top of that, I received evaluations that were completely inconsistent. Then when I viewed the ratings and comments, I contacted my lawyer. The lawyer helped me construct memorandums to give him, but the principal kept ignoring them after multiple times of me trying to discuss how he rated me on my performance. I have no respect for him and as another retired faculty member said of him, he is all about "self-preservation."

Why should I let these people and circumstances make me feel so bad about myself and about life? It's not worth it! It was never the teaching part that I disliked. It was all of the other "stuff." It's a miracle with all of this stress added to my life, that I made it 18 years.

Beyond the Bell Bonus Tip:

Think about all the "stuff" in your job that has happened to you and decide if you have an escalating snowball.

I WAS TIRED

You often feel tired, not because you've done too much, but because you've done too little of what sparks a light in you.

~Alexander den Heijer

I know you are tired, but you have to keep going.

~Addaxmo

Life it too short for a workplace environment that

depletes and diminishes you.

~Ken Coleman

Being a teacher is exhausting … mentally, emotionally, and physically. The demands are overwhelming. And it doesn't stop as soon as the kids get on the bus to go home, or when school lets out for the summer. Honestly, I was tired of being tired.

I was tired of being unhappy. I was tired of leaving work and feeling like I had been run over by a Mack Truck. I was tired of looking frazzled and drained. I remember one day going into the local post office after work and one of the employees there asking, "Are you okay?" because I looked so distraught from a typical day at work.

I was tired of how my job and administrators made me feel. I was tired of being treated as incompetent. I was tired of a job that had me lacking self-confidence and feeling like I had to always defend myself. I was tired of walking on eggshells filled with anxiety waiting for someone to tell me something else I was doing wrong. I was tired of feeling beaten down, feeling picked on, single out, and substandard. I was tired of the resentment and lack of respect. I was tired of living like my head was always just above water.

I was tired of feeling overwhelmed, fatigued, stressed, and frustrated. I was tired of taking anxiety pills before leaving for work just to be able to deal with work on a daily basis. I was tired of taking de-stress gummies at 7:00 each morning. I was tired of contemplating putting in a catheter for the school year because I didn't have time to go to the bathroom. I was tired of not feeling good enough. I was tired of doing the job of three people. I was tired up shoving Vaseline up my nose to prevent daily nose bleeds before putting on my face mask.

I was tired of feeling like a yo-yo when I might have a couple of good days or a good week or two in a row, and then something bad would happen again.

I was tired of wearing faculty T-shirts and buying more grade level T-shirts and dressing up in silly tutus for spirit day and costumes on book character day. I craved respect and being treated like an adult.

I had come to the point where I was wondering why I was doing all of this work and dealing with all of this stress, for what? It certainly wasn't the money. All of this for a low-paying job with little to no respect? I feel like public education as a whole is messed up. Teachers do not have the support they need. Even with attorneys, it is the admin's agenda, and they don't genuinely care about how you feel, unless they like you.

I was tired of always being on the countdown to the next holiday, the next day off, or the weekend. I was tired of looking for the next break. I was tired of just merely existing. I was tired of working at a soul-sucking job. I was tired of being tired. I began questioning myself: What am I doing? What kind of life is this? I finally decided I deserved better than this. The turmoil I was going through was not worth it. Enough is enough. I put my foot down and told myself I wasn't going to let another year go by without pursuing a different career.

Beyond the Bell Bonus Tip:

Make a list of what you are tired of in your career.

PRAY

"For I know the plans I have for you," declares the Lord.
"Plans to prosper you, and not to harm you. Plans to give you
hope and a future."

~Jeremiah 29:11

Let go and let God.

~Unknown

But he said to me, "My grace is sufficient for you, for my power
is made perfect in weakness."

~2 Corinthians 12:9

Before making my decision to leave the classroom, I began taking a long look at my life. Where I had come from, what I had gone through, and where I was going. I didn't like the road ahead. This was not my purpose-driven life. I knew God would not want me living my life in this way, which was full of worry and fear, anxiety, and stress.

I knew I was made for more than this. I knew I had a bigger purpose. I had let a job and everything it entails consume me, and I didn't like who I had become. I wasn't happy with my life. I knew there was more to life than grading papers and recess duty. And I knew I deserved better. There was more to life than this. I knew I wasn't living God's best.

I spent a lot of time in prayer. God and I had many talks. I prayed when I woke up. I prayed on the way to school. I prayed at school. I prayed at night before bed. I prayed for clarity, peace, and direction. I prayed for growth and the right connections to cross my path. I prayed that God would open new doors of opportunity that he had planned for just me. I was in constant prayer for breakthroughs.

It reminded me of a sermon I listened to a while back. The pastor told the story of a man who dies and goes to Heaven. And when he got there, he asked God why he didn't give him certain things in his lifetime. And God replied, "Because you didn't ask." God had created all of these blessings for him. God was simply waiting for the man to ask for them. I don't want to be the person who misses out simply because I did not ask.

So, I asked that God lead me where He wanted me to go. And that he would give a sign—something so crystal clear that I couldn't miss it. That the right job would land in my lap. Almost like a gift that He handed to me and said, "Calley, this is for you."

I was a disaster, and I just handed it over to Him. And I asked him to create something wonderful out of my mess. I let go of a lot of things and gave it to God. I had to trust God fully.

Once I was able to do that, I thanked God that He was making a way for me, even though I couldn't see it at the time. I didn't know where my future would lead, but I knew who was leading it.

I ended up connecting with a family member whom I had not seen in years. He kept in constant contact with me through phone and text. He became my prayer partner through this transition. If I had something going on at work, I could also send him a message and count on him to pray for me and give me scripture or words of encouragement.

Once I took the limits off of God, I began living with expectancy. My life started turning around. God started exceeding my expectations. Everything started aligning. Everything was starting to fall into place. I was beginning to get what I had prayed for.

Beyond the Bell Bonus Tip:

Leap, and the net will appear.
~John Burroughs

How I Knew It Was Time to Leave

A good rule of thumb is that any environment that consistently leaves you feeling bad about who you are is the wrong environment.

~Laurie Helgoe

You're killing yourself for a job that would replace you within a week if you dropped dead. Take care of yourself.

~Unknown

People don't leave bad jobs ... they leave because of bad bosses, poor management, who don't appreciate their value.

~Unknown

For years, I knew I needed to get out of the classroom. I knew I needed to explore other options. My decision and these feelings didn't happen overnight. This was years and years of stress and misery building. But the year Covid hit was the tip of the iceberg. I had discussed this with my friend, Kim, many times. She has always been so supportive of me and encouraged me to look into other careers. But when I finally decided this would be my last year, she jokingly said, "It took a pandemic!" as if this were the final push I needed.

In March 2020, our school shut down due to Covid, and my state was on lockdown to slow the spread of the virus. It was very challenging because we were told to take everything home with us that we would need to teach. From mid-March until the end of May, I worked from home, and this was how I finished the school year. It was so sad. This was one of my most favorite classes and I did not even get the chance to properly say goodbye to them.

School started back in August and because the virus was still rampant, I didn't expect us to stay in school face-to-face for very long. In the back of my mind, I was secretly hoping that the virus would cause the school to shut down and I could work from home, which would eliminate 90% of my problems and what was causing so much stress. But when the school didn't shut down for Covid, I prayed for a blizzard, or at the very least a snow day, anything that would allow me to be at home.

Teaching is already more than a full-time job. The responsibility teachers have is overwhelming. But with the pandemic, the responsibilities doubled, and I felt like I had two full-time jobs. More work piled on. My school system started with masks being optional in the classroom, but required during transitions, and then when cases started to rise, we went to a full mask mandate for everyone, all day, except when eating or drinking. I felt like I was on mask patrol all day, making sure students were wearing them properly and not below their chin or slinging food in them in the lunchroom like a slingshot, which actually did happen.

I kept seven clipboards going at all times just to keep track of all of my responsibilities. I had one for lesson plans, one for my guided reading group, one for transportation changes students might have, like car rider or riding a different bus, one to keep my grades on, another for my temperature log, another to track my communication with parents, and a daily checklist to make sure I got everything done that had to be completed during the day.

Many days I didn't eat lunch. I didn't have time. I was too busy checking email, responding to parents' texts, grading work, attending virtual meetings to help students who were at home, gathering books to send to the office for students who were in quarantine, putting grades in the computer, and managing makeup work that students finally decided to do that had been assigned two months before. Other days I realized as soon as I got the kids on the bus that I had not gone to the bathroom since about 7:20 that morning. I felt so unhealthy.

I was having to manage seating charts, which changed daily depending on whether students were face-to-face or virtual, temperature logs, cleaning up breakfast in the classroom every morning, lunch in the classroom twice a week, toting books and materials back and forth to my home for virtual days on Fridays. I was teaching virtual and face-to-face at the same time. I couldn't keep up with everything, between face-to-face students and virtual students and not sure who had Covid, who was quarantined, or who just decided to be virtual for the day. I couldn't keep track of how many face-to-face kids I had each day. I counted and recounted so I would know in case we had our monthly fire drill. Makeup work was a nightmare, and it didn't help that my school allowed students makeup work anytime during the nine-week grading period. So basically, if an assignment was assigned in August, students could turn it in sometime in October. A lot of students didn't have any parental support and weren't even doing their work on virtual days. But who do you think got blamed for kids not doing their work or for failing?

I wasn't happy with administration at my school. My principal was a control freak and micromanaged everything! I felt like I was walking on eggshells all the time around them. I felt scrutinized and harassed on a daily basis. In fact, one of my administrators conducted two observations on me in one day!

I recall one teacher who got observed consecutively in the same week and was concerned about it because why would a veteran teacher need multiple observations conducted in the same week? When she brought it to the principal's attention, he threw his authority around and said that he could come in and observe as many times as he wanted. Many times I felt harassed and interrogated. I felt like I was doing something wrong all the time. I felt like I couldn't please anyone or was always being watched or trying to find a mistake with something I was doing. Admin had their favorites and treated others differently depending on who you were. They acted like they wanted to help everyone, but this was not the case. Because everyone was under so much stress due to Covid, admin even offered for the faculty to come up to their office and shut the door and come talk to them about anything, but I would be afraid they would either write me up or hold what I said against me. Favoritism was rampant, especially to those who brown-nosed and didn't question their motives or leadership. We've all heard the famous quote, "There is no reality, only perception." Some people may disagree and say, "No, that is only your perception." I'm sorry to disagree, but my perception is my reality.

I disagreed with how certain things were run at the school. Some decisions they made went completely against my moral compass. So almost every day, I had to bite my tongue because I felt like what I had to say didn't matter. Administration had their own agenda. I knew it would not matter what I said or how I felt—it wasn't going to change anything, and they didn't want to hear about it anyway. It was all about whatever they could do to make themselves look better or make the school look better to the community.

I believed that these kids would leave our school feeling like the world owed them something. I didn't feel like we were setting up our students for success in the real world. Students would think they were entitled, and that everything in life is fair and there are no consequences. One example was when we had a fundraiser at our school. The top earners were to be awarded snow cones as an incentive. Instead of giving the students who worked hard to either get donations or sell items, they just decided to award everyone a snow cone. How is that right? And how did the students who worked hard feel when the students who did nothing earned the same reward? Admin wanted everything to be happy and positive, which is great, but it isn't realistic. Another example was another snow cone incident. We had the Kona Ice Man truck come and students were able to purchase a snow cone, but if they didn't have money, they still received one. A student who was in "time out" due to biting a student the previous day was also given this reward. I feel like this student, who left bite marks that turned black and blue on another student, should not receive a treat, especially when they were removed from the class to stay in "time out" somewhere else. What are we teaching these kids? I felt like we weren't teaching students responsibility and accountability for their choices and actions. Some of their decisions went completely against my ethics and morals.

In 18 years with multiple principals, I had never been in "trouble" in my school system until this year. And it came from someone who had never even taught before! I lost all respect for him. I felt like I was being watched, almost to the point of harassment. I just wanted them to leave me alone. I tried to lay low and get out as fast as I could. He felt that it would benefit me in my professional development by going and observing a high school teacher, although I'm not sure how. It was a completely different age group and setting to even try to compare. This teacher had a total of eight students and an hour-and-a-half block of time to teach them six math problems. And then he decided he wanted me to meet with him and another admin for "book club" once a week to discuss a book on teaching and a couple of articles he printed and had me reflect on how it was going to make me a better teacher. He started our weekly "meetings" with small talk. You know, asking how I was and how my weekend went. Like they cared anyway! And frankly, it was none of their business. I usually answered in one-word responses. We met almost every week from January to April. And he made a point to tell me that he had ordered me my very own copy of the book so I could write notes and highlight in it. It was the biggest joke and waste of my time. Don't get me wrong, I like professional development and learning and growing. I like learning more about myself and how it applies to my position, but when this is presented to you by someone you do not like or respect, and as a means of singling me out and belittling me, I'm not going to get anything out of it. It felt like more of an interrogation than reflection. All I was doing was jumping through hoops to suffice the demands, so I basically just shook my head and agreed to everything they said about the book. I did whatever I could do to get the admin off my back. You should have heard the people I told laugh at the absurdity of it. They couldn't believe they were making me read a book and reflect on how it was going to change my life and how it was supposed to make me a better teacher. Not to mention that I disagreed with most of what the book said. It was almost as ridiculous as what they did to a teacher who retired last year.

She had 30 years of teaching experience, was retiring that year, and they felt that she needed a mentor. Are you kidding me? Who does that? What kind of leader is that? And how humiliating to be leaving your career with a mentor because the admin, one of which has not even taught a day in his life, felt she needed one. Oh, and if you are wondering what I did with the "book club" book ... as I am writing this, the jury is still out on whether to use it for fire starter or toilet paper.

As if it weren't stressful enough, I got an email from my admin getting onto me and another teacher because students threw trash in the wrong trash can! Are you kidding me? They should be excited students actually put trash in a trashcan. I had parents on many occasions texting and emailing on Friday nights at 10 p.m. asking about their child's performance, grades, or turning in makeup work, or other times over the weekend about questions that could have easily been asked on Monday morning. There was such a lack of respect for me and my time. I felt as though each day I was going into battle. Battle against administration, disengaged parents, and disruptive students.

In early fall, I hit my breaking point. I found myself crying at home on the floor in the fetal position. The toxic work environment made me feel trapped. I felt like it was my first year teaching all over again. I felt broken. I was emotionally exhausted. I was undervalued. I was bursting at the seams. I ended up going to multiple doctor appointments and ended up on meds to cope. Essentially, I was diagnosed with depression and anxiety from my job and work environment. Thankfully, he helped me get it under control, at least to the point where it was manageable. Your body will tell you when it is time to move on.

On April 1 (April Fools' of all days), and two days before spring break so I would have time to process over the break (wasn't that so thoughtful?!), my principal decided to call me into his office and tell me that I still had a job the next year and I would have a contract, but my job would be teaching at a different school and teaching second grade. They said they needed a certain "skill set" in that grade. That's funny, especially since I'd never taught second grade, and they wouldn't tell me what that skill set was. They said it was a "district" decision. That's funny because the district had never observed me teach, yet they felt that I would be better in a primary age level when I'd taught 17 years at the elementary age? I'm sure it had more to do with me calling my lawyer about him all year than it did about my "skill set." And I had found a teacher that I worked really well with—everything from sharing similar ideas to lesson planning, but they decided to break up our team (he decided to send her to first grade), but other people in our school who worked well together, they wouldn't dare separate. I had already lost all respect for him, but this was the icing on the cake. I simply said, "Okay," and it fueled me even more to find another job. They thought I was going to go to second grade, but what they didn't know was that I had been planning my escape since fall.

During post-planning, I went to my "new" school to finish out my remaining days. I tried to do as little as possible because I knew I was not going to return the following year. So, while everyone else was getting their rooms ready, I used the excuse that I just didn't know what theme I wanted for next year or how I wanted to decorate my room. I attended meetings and helped clean out a storage closet, but other than that, I did very little prep work for the classroom.

My life was out of balance. I felt like I didn't have a life outside of work. I didn't trust but a few people who I worked with. I didn't admire the people above me. But through the mistreatment and stress, I channeled my energy into finding a way out.

I decided to leave for a number of reasons. A lot of it from things that had built up over time. I felt like it was a combination of burnout, differences with decision-makers and their decisions not aligning with my vision, and just ready for something more. At times I had thought about teaching at another school, but I had gone through so much, I was just done. I felt like this career was holding me back. But ultimately it came down to my health and happiness that were being compromised.

Beyond the Bell Bonus Tip:

When your job negatively affects your health and happiness, it's time to get out.

MOVE IN SILENCE

Work hard in silence. Let your success be your noise.

~Frank Ocean

Nobody knew I was getting a new car until I pulled up on them.
Nobody knew I got another job until they saw my work badge.
Nobody knew I was moving until I got my keys. Moral of the
story: Move in Silence.

~Cece Symone

Don't ever mistake my silence for ignorance, my calmness for
acceptance, and my kindness for weakness.

~Dalai Lama

Throughout this process I stayed quiet. I moved in silence. Only a select few people knew I was making a career change. I shared with them what I was interested in doing and some of the steps I was taking to achieve it.

I didn't want anyone to know. I kept it private for several reasons. One reason is I'm a pretty private person. It was no one's business anyway. Another reason was, at this point, I was on a leg of the journey where I was still trying to figure out the career path I would take. I also didn't want anyone in my school, especially the admin, to know because they would have someone hired before I turned in my resignation letter.

I think moving in silence is a good idea. By doing this, you are taking steps to something bigger in your life, but you are not announcing your progress to the world. It preserves what you want and what you are working to achieve.

Moving in silence gives you a competitive edge. In this situation, you are making a new life for yourself that others probably want for themselves, but don't know how to go about achieving it. By keeping silent, you are keeping other competition or "players" from getting wind of what you are doing. By keeping your initiatives under wraps, you are ahead of possible competitors.

I think sharing with a close friend or two is a good idea, just because we all want to share big things going on in our lives. It's hard to keep that big of a change a secret. It feels good to have someone to talk to, especially at the beginning phases of a transition. If your plan is just on the horizon, it's exciting to share ideas with others and receive feedback. These few friends could also serve as accountability partners, keeping you on track with the ultimate goal. Not only that, but they can celebrate small wins along the way with you. And by only telling a few people, it's easier to explain if your plans happen to change, or some things don't go as planned, or some other factor causes a delay, or if you even happen to fail (as failure is very real and happens to us all). That way, other people are not critiquing you, but you have your small group of support to provide positivity and help encourage you as you re-strategize.

Beyond the Bell Bonus Tip:

Keep your next move to yourself.

THINGS ARE LOOKING UP

I am learning to love the sound of my feet walking away from things not meant for me.

~A.G.

Your next step will become clear the moment you bravely begin to walk towards what your heart is calling you to do.

~Annmarie Molina

But still, like dust, I'll rise.

~Maya Angelou

At the end of the day, all you need is hope and strength. Hope that it will get better, and strength to hold on until it does.

~Unknown

After I made my decision to leave, things began to change. And change for the better.

I stopped crying. I stopped caring about things that I was about to leave behind. I stopped letting things get to me. Yes, I still had bad days, but they didn't affect me nearly as much because I knew I only had a short time left and I would be out for good.

I was happier, had more confidence, and started to feel like myself again. I knew I was on the right path. And I knew I had made the right decision.

I could then focus my energy on figuring a way out, laying the groundwork, and paving a path for my new future. I was constantly on the countdown. I had five months left. Then it was 43 days. And before I knew it, I was down to three more weeks.

I remember in December I had texted my friend Kim what path I had decided to take. And how excited I was that I had made so many new connections, that my new career would offer more money and less stress, and about how good I felt. She said to me, "That is the best Christmas gift for peace of mind for you." I hadn't really thought of it like that, but she was right! Merry Christmas to me!

Because I could now see light at the end of the tunnel, I no longer felt trapped.

The best part of my days was job searching, receiving emails from companies who wanted to get to know me better, adding to my portfolio, and updating my resume on new skills I had learned. This kept me going each and every day.

When companies emailed me wanting me to meet or discuss a job or project, it was the complete opposite of school, where they only wanted to meet with me to tell me something else that I was doing wrong.

Beyond the Bell Bonus Tip:
Keep your chin up!

How to Survive Until You Can Get Out

*When everything seems to be going against you, remember that
the airplane takes off against the wind, not with it.*

~Henry Ford

*Hardships often prepare ordinary people for an extraordinary
destiny.*

~C.S. Lewis

Storms make trees take deeper roots.

~Dolly Parton

Discovering new job postings, hearing back from companies, and them inviting me to schedule interviews, is what got me through most days.

I also had a coworker who was looking to leave education as well. Our conversations, looking at job descriptions, and updating our resumes and portfolios was the highlight of my day. It kept me going.

I wanted to leave so badly. I had to channel my frustration. I did so by using that energy to keep up my job search and applying to job postings.

During this time of "survival," try to visualize how your life will change for the better once you do leave and when you finally get out. It's a lot of work, but it will be so worth it!

Make sure you have an accountability partner that you can "check in" with on a regular basis. This will help you move forward, one step at a time.

Also, keep yourself healthy. Have regular health checks, especially if you have had stress-related symptoms.

The next several chapters go into more depth as to what you can do to be good to yourself and keep your sanity until you can get out.

Beyond the Bell Bonus Tip:

Find something to look forward to that will keep you motivated.

GET A VISION

What you choose to focus on becomes your reality.

~Jen Sincero

Where there is no vision the people perish.

~Proverbs 29:18

Our culture has been fed the lie for far too long that work isn't meant to be meaningful or satisfying.

~Ken Coleman

You are about to embark on a new journey! It's time to get a clear vision on what you want in your new job.

You need to get clear on what you were created to do. And not only that, but get certain on how you want to feel about your day-to-day life. What do you want for yourself? What works best for your family? What do you want for your future?

You want to find a job you will enjoy. So, you need to get some clarity on what you feel like you do best. What makes you thrive? What do you enjoy doing the most? What kind of work engages you? What are you most passionate about doing? What interests do you have that excite you? Do you have interest in topics that you like to learn about in your spare time?

Once you figure out these internal specifics, then begin looking for a job that meets your other wants and needs.

In order to get started looking for a job or a new career change, it might be a good idea to make a list of what you want and what you need. What are your must-haves and where are you willing to compromise? When you are transitioning to a new job, you may want to consider some of the following:

- Will you work at another school, an office, or remotely?
- Do you need to move?
- Will you need insurance and benefits, or will your spouse be providing those?
- Do you want to go back to school for an advanced degree?
- Will you need further education?
- Will you need certificates?
- Will you need to obtain a license?
- Do you want to work full-time or part-time?
- Do you want to do freelance work or contract positions?
- Are you willing to work weekends?
- How much flexibility do you need?
- Are you willing to work different shifts?
- When are you leaving teaching? Mid-year? Next month? In two weeks? At the end of the year?

For my particular situation I had a pretty good idea of what I wanted and needed. As far as what the career change needed was to offer me more chances for growth and opportunity. As a teacher, there aren't many opportunities, unless you want to go into administration, and that was not something I was even remotely interested in. I wanted to continue learning and applying my skills I had acquired in all of my years of teaching.

I knew I had signed a contract (at the beginning of my search) with my district, and if at all possible, I wanted to finish that contract and not break it. I told myself that if I found something, I was willing to begin with a part-time job or contract work, something I could do on nights and weekends, but the plan was to go full-time in the summer.

I'm single, so I am the only breadwinner in my family. I don't have another income or anyone else to depend on financially. I knew that I was not willing to take a commission-only position because I needed the steady income. I was not willing to take a pay cut. I needed to make at least what I was making with my teacher salary but would welcome a higher salary.

I knew that I did not want to go back to school for another degree. I already had my six-year college credentials, and I was not interested in doing another master's program or getting my doctorate.

I knew I wanted a full-time job. I knew I needed health, dental, and life insurance. I also wanted something that offered retirement. I enjoy having my weekends free, so that meant I wanted a Monday to Friday position. I also wanted to work fully remotely. I live in a small town with not many job opportunities, and I'm not really at a point in my life where I am looking to move.

Just as important as salary expectations and benefits, I wanted freedom. I wanted flexibility. I wanted to have less stress and be happier. I wanted to use the skills I acquired and what I was best at in the classroom and use those in a new role. I wanted to drink as much water as I wanted and be able to go to the bathroom whenever I needed without asking someone to cover my class. I wanted to eat lunch uninterrupted and actually chew my food instead of swallowing it whole while checking email, returning a phone call, answering a text, and grading papers. I wanted to be treated like an adult and not like a tall child. I wanted to be treated with respect. I wanted to work in a climate that made me feel valued and appreciated. I wanted to look forward to going to work.

I also wanted a corporate position. After much research, it seemed like a better fit for me, not to mention better pay. Corporate companies want you to be happy. They thrive on their job ratings and overall culture and climate. If you are happy, then you are going to provide better quality work for them. Unlike in school systems where they don't really care because they assume you're not going anywhere no matter how bad it gets because they think you can't find any other jobs with a teaching certificate.

I knew what I was asking for. And I knew I deserved it. I also realized that just because I wanted or needed something in my new career, did not mean I would necessarily get it. But if I found something that checked most of my boxes, then I was going to go for it. It is challenging to find a job that meets every single criteria I had in mind, but it gave me a good starting point. I might not find a job that meets everything I wrote on my list, but then again, I might. So, I focused mainly on the job postings that offered what I was looking for.

By envisioning what you want and what you don't want, it will help you get a clearer picture of what jobs to look for. It will help you narrow down the search.

I believe we become what we constantly think about. I changed my focus to what I envisioned for myself and where I wanted my life to go.

I started talking about my future. I started talking to my future. I made statements like, "When I leave…," **not** IF I leave. I challenge you to do the same.

Beyond the Bell Bonus Tip:

Think outside of the box in terms of what you want your future life to look like.

PACE YOURSELF

*You'll never grow in your career or your life if you're not
intentionally taking steps to do so.*

~Ken Coleman

*You're not going to master the rest of your life in one day. Just
relax. Master the day. Then just keep doing that every day.*

~Unknown

Changing careers is a big deal. And it can get overwhelming. But making even small moves toward your goal will make it manageable and not feel so overpowering.

Set small attainable goals to show your progress. Make a to-do list and start checking it off. The more checks you have, the more motivated you will stay.

It could be as simple as goals for the day, goals for the week, goals for the month. Below are some examples of actions you could do.

Goals for the day:

- ⊙ Research career opportunities
- ⊙ Sign up for job alerts
- ⊙ Watch a podcast
- ⊙ Apply to 10 jobs

Goals for the week:

- ⊙ Schedule two interviews
- ⊙ Update your resume
- ⊙ Create a cover letter
- ⊙ Connect with 100 people on LinkedIn

Goals for the month:

- ⊙ Learn a new tool
- ⊙ Apply a new skill
- ⊙ Create a portfolio
- ⊙ Read an inspiring book

Beyond the Bell Bonus Tip:

Take small steps to keep you on track. By doing a little at a time and pacing yourself, you won't be so overwhelmed.

GET BUSY

Procrastination is the thief of time, collar him.

~Charles Dickens

*If you want to conquer fear, don't sit home and think about it.
Go out and get busy.*

~Dale Carnegie

*People talk about caterpillars becoming butterflies as though they
just go into a cocoon, slap on wings, and are good to go.
Caterpillars have to dissolve into a disgusting pile of goo to
become butterflies. So if you're a mess wrapped up in blankets
right now, keep going.*

~Jennifer Wright

I was so busy learning, growing, looking for new possibilities, I was transitioning before my own eyes. It was such an exciting time!

I had so many other interests and responsibilities going on, I barely had time for my full-time teaching job. It was like my day job was getting in the way of my future. I couldn't wait to get home to learn or watch a new podcast or finish up a module on a class I was taking. Or I was working on my cover letter, resume, or portfolio. Or applying to new companies from job posts. I had hundreds of job posting alerts emailed to me each week. It took hours to sift through each one. And if I didn't review the job postings daily, I would get so behind and bogged down. When you barely have time for your day job, you know you are doing something right!

I was excited to see how many connections I had made with people from the same field I was trying to get in. I enjoyed reading their posts and getting emails from people all over the world. I was also constantly finding something to read or watch or signing up for more newsletters that may help me in some way.

The highlight of my day was adding a new skill I had learned to my resume, applying to jobs, getting emails from companies wanting interviews, or hearing that I made it to the next round of interviews.

I was exhausted, but I was channeling that in a way that gave life back to me because I was working on my future. That was my motivator.

I knew it would be uncomfortable for a short while, and then the hard work was going to pay off. I knew the busyness would be temporary, but the payoff would affect the rest of my life. It was simply a season.

For several weeks I was so exhausted from trying to keep everything going while working a full-time job, that I had to take breaks for a few days. I felt guilty, but I knew I needed a break because I felt like I was wearing myself thin. Give yourself some grace. Do what you need to do to recharge so you can get back at it.

Be prepared for your life to be crazier than normal for a while. But also reassure yourself that it is temporary and the reason you are doing all of this is a pretty darn good one! The work you put in now will help set the stage for your future. Be prepared to go through a metamorphosis and anticipate the person you are becoming.

Beyond the Bell Bonus Tip:
Sign up for job alerts in the field you're interested in!

SHIFT YOUR MINDSET

Our happiness depends on the habit of mind we cultivate. So practice happy thinking every day. Cultivate the merry heart, develop the happiness habit, and life will become a continual feast.

~Norman Vincent Peale

Train your mind to see the good in everything. Positivity is a choice. The happiness of your life depends on the quality of your thoughts.

~Unknown

In order to transition from teaching or any other career, you must have a growth mindset. This simply means that you believe in yourself and your abilities to change, adapt, learn, develop, and grow. If you are actively seeking learning opportunities, you will more likely have greater success in your career search and when you actually land your new job.

You are about to encounter new challenges and changes. Be open to learning and continuing to learn because things are always evolving.

Having a growth mindset helps you overcome hurdles along the way and shows persistence. Jumping into a new career is a lot of work, especially if you are coming from a career you have been in for many years. It's hard to shift your normal patterns and thinking. You are not going to know how to do everything perfectly the first, second, or even third attempt in a new job. But by using what you have and what you have learned, your skills and talents can be further developed.

Try to not let feelings of doubt and insecurity get in the way. Many times, we ask ourselves, "Do I have the skills?" or "Do I have what it takes to perform this task?" Because we sometimes doubt ourselves and our abilities, it deters us from actually trying.

Instead of asking, "What if I don't get hired in a new position?" we need to change our way of thinking.

Instead, try asking:

- ⊙ What if I leave and I'm happier?
- ⊙ What if I make a transition and I become healthier?
- ⊙ What if I resign and make more money?
- ⊙ What if I choose a new career option and experience less stress and a better quality of life?

Beyond the Bell Bonus Tip:

By making these small changes, it will create big results. Not only will you notice, but so will your future employer.

SEEK BALANCE

Life is a balance between what we can control and what we cannot. I am learning to live between effort and surrender.

~Danielle Orner

Balance isn't fitting everything in. It's starting with what's important and letting the rest fall as it will.

~Erica Layne

Balance is not something you find, it's something you create.

~Jana Kingsford

The key to keeping your balance is knowing when you've lost it.

~Unknown

My life was not in balance, and I suffered for it. For me, I need my time split up into segments. I need time alone, time with friends and family, time to reflect, time for exercise, time for the outdoors, and time for rest. I like to cut my time into sections similar to a pie chart, and when that chart was not cut equally, I suffered.

Having balance does not mean everything is perfect. When you are balanced, you are able to better deal with the stresses of life. You are able to better manage it. When I feel balanced, I feel more efficient and more productive.

Finding balance can be simple, if you make time to make it intentional. Make sure you have balance for work, fun, family, personal time, and relationships.

Ways to find balance:

1-Get rid of the clutter—Remove anything that isn't serving you. This could mean things around your house, and it could also mean people in your life.

2-Know your priorities—This means for tomorrow, next week, and two years down the road. What is of most importance, significant, and has a sense of urgency?

3-Leave work at work—Make a conscious effort to not bring work home. However, if you work from home, put parameters on when it is "work" time and "home" time.

4-Listen to your body—This could mean getting enough exercise, eating the right food, knowing when you need a break, or need to rest. Your body will tell you if you simply listen.

5-Do something you love every day—It could be as simple as reading a book, calling a friend, or cuddling with your puppy.

Beyond the Bell Bonus Tip:

If we find time to keep balance, we are better able to handle change. And big change is what you are about to experience!

SET YOUR BOUNDARIES

Love yourself enough to set boundaries. Your time and energy are precious. You get to choose how you use it. You teach people how to treat you by deciding what you will and won't accept.

~Anna Taylor

Boundaries are your responsibility. You decide what is and isn't allowed in your life.

~Brittney Moses

A lack of boundaries often invites a lack of respect.

~Toby Mac

Boundaries: If someone throws a fit because you set boundaries, it's just more evidence the boundary is needed.

~Unknown

A boundary is an invisible barrier between yourself and others. Boundaries are the limits and rules we set for ourselves and our relationships.

Boundaries limit what you will do or put up with, and also serve as a line that others may not cross. They protect you. They also preserve your time and sense of self.

Boundaries are important because they empower you. They allow you to say no when you need to. They allow you to let go of things that are not in your best interest. By setting boundaries, we teach others how to respect us and our space.

Setting boundaries is up to you. You decide what you will accept and what you will not. You set your parameters and adjust as necessary.

Setting boundaries during this time of transition is important and crucial because they protect you from others encroaching on your personal life.

Learn to say "No." You don't owe anyone a reason or explanation.

Beyond the Bell Bonus Tip:

Remember that "No" is a complete sentence.

DO NOT COMPARE YOURSELF TO OTHERS

For we dare not make ourselves of the number, or compare ourselves with some that commend themselves: but they measuring themselves by themselves, and comparing themselves among themselves, are not wise.

~2 Corinthians 10:12

Comparison is the thief of joy.

~Theodore Roosevelt

A flower does not think of competing to the flower next to it. It just blooms.

~Zen Shin

Comparison is the death of all joy, and the only person you need to be better than is the one you were yesterday.

~Rachel Hollis

If we are comparing ourselves and our stories to others, then we aren't really focusing on our own self because we are distracted by others' progress. I ran into this a lot on my journey. I was guilty of comparing myself to other people.

I'm a member of a lot of social media groups that are geared for teachers that are for support and helping teachers find a way into another field or career path. I've spent hours reading many of the stories that were posted, both good and bad.

At times it was difficult to read some of the stories of people who had already left teaching. Some teachers had posted that they just turned in their resignation letter and it was only November. Or some who had already turned in their resignation letter and would not be returning the following year. While I was happy for them and celebrated their success, it was also difficult not to be a bit jealous that they had already achieved what I was working toward. I had to constantly remind myself that everyone had a different journey. And while the goal may be the same, the path was going to be different for all of us.

I knew I would reach my goal, just not exactly sure how or when. The same is true for you. Just because it hasn't happened yet doesn't mean that it won't. You are on your way, and you will get there.

Keep pushing forward. You will arrive at your destination when you are meant to. It may take more twists and turns than you expect. Don't worry if others are further along or going about it a different way.

It's not a race. Focus on yourself and reaching your goals. Take one day at a time. Celebrate and learn from others. Before long, your story will be inspiring others. Focus on yourself during this time, so later you can help others achieve what you are about to.

Beyond the Bell Bonus Tip:
Focus on yourself and your journey.

SELF-CARE

Keep taking time for yourself until you're you again.

~Lalah Delia

I have come to believe that caring for myself is not self-indulgent.
Caring for myself is an act of survival.

~Audre Lorde

During this time of change and transition, I found it to be extremely essential to be good to myself. I already had enough unknowns and alterations going on in my life to deal with, not to mention the stress of my job, so I wanted to take care of myself. I knew this was important because I wouldn't be as focused on job searches and interviews without some serenity and self-love.

I knew I needed to focus on my mental, physical, social, and emotional well-being. When I got home from work, I wanted to decompress and do anything I could to bring stress relief.

For my mental health, I spent time reading books. I had an extensive list in my Amazon shopping cart. And I had books on reserve from my local library. They ranged in topics from wealth and money, to spirituality, to adventure, and everything in between. I also spent a lot of time learning. I will forever be a lifelong learner, and I spent my time learning new skills that would help me in my next career. I also got organized. I cleaned out most of the things in the house that were clutter and taking up space. This orderliness was a tangible way to help clear my mind and get rid of distractions.

For my physical well-being, I focused on getting healthier. I drank more water, or at least I did when I was at home or on the weekends when I could actually get to the bathroom without asking anyone to watch my class. I exercised, mostly hiking with my dog, or taking walks with my mom. I love being outdoors and getting fresh air.

For my social well-being, I got together with friends, planned outings and dinner get-togethers. I needed that socialization and to be able to laugh and have adult conversations. But I also learned to say "no" to some of the extra things coming up, like events or parties, and things that would end up draining me of more energy.

Emotionally, I craved tranquility and calmness. I first turned my bathroom into a spa-like retreat. It was an oasis. I spent a small fortune on expensive candles, bath bombs, and bottles of bubble bath. I purchased a luxurious robe and had it monogrammed with my initials. I bought new clothes and shoes, not that I needed them, but a new outfit never hurts. I indulged in the occasional spa day. It did wonders for my soul.

When you are good to yourself, it shows up in other aspects of your life. Put yourself first when you can.

Beyond the Bell Bonus Tip:

Remember that self-care is not selfish; it is necessary.

EXPLORE

If someone offers you an amazing opportunity and you're not sure you can do it, say yes, then learn how to do it later.

~Richard Branson

Your passion is the kind of work that would make them come alive every morning.

~Ken Coleman

Look for the job that you would take if you didn't need a job.

~Warren Buffet

I want you to think back to what you wanted to be when you were growing up. Did you want to be an astronaut? Firefighter? Doctor? I'm not sure why we are expected to know what we want to do with the rest of our lives by the time we turn 18 years old.

Maybe you got into the education field and have now decided it is not for you. That is OKAY! You have lots of other options. And yes, I did say OPTIONS, plural—more than one!

Take the time to explore what is out there. Find what makes you tick. What is your sweet spot? When are you your best self? What are you passionate about? What makes you feel alive? What would make you happy? What would make you feel like it isn't even work?

Even if you are a few years into your career, or about to retire, explore other jobs and opportunities. Maybe there are some aspects about teaching you don't like, but you may find another career that lets you do the things you love about teaching without the things you dislike about it.

Now is the time to rediscover yourself. Even if you've only taught three years, you have changed and grown as a person. Maybe now you realize your best direction and where you want your life to go. Maybe it is a completely different field. Or maybe it is only a small adjustment to the skills you already know and have developed. Maybe you know that you need more flexibility, a better work-life balance, more financial opportunities and security.

Put yourself out there and see what is available to you. And don't feel guilty that you didn't know what you wanted by the time you finished high school.

Beyond the Bell Bonus Tip:

While you are exploring what is out there, remember "you're not starting from scratch— you're starting from experience." (Unknown)

LEVEL UP

You'll climb faster and further by surrounding yourself with people who are focused, driven, and motivated to reach their own goals.

~Ken Coleman

Surround yourself with people who force you to level up.

~Unknown

You are only going to be as good as the people you surround yourself with so be brave enough to let go of those who keep weighing you down.

~Ziad K. Abdelnour

Most people don't pursue their dreams because they're surrounded by others who aren't pursuing their dreams.

~Ken Coleman

By leveling up, you are improving your current situation and increasing your stature in life. The first step is making the decision to do it. Then identify your available resources to help you achieve your goal. People, friends, connections, and acquaintances are part of your resources. Utilize them!

Surround yourself with what you want. Surround yourself with what you're going after. Surround yourself with your future. What do I mean by that? I mean that you need to be around and spend time with people who push you to be your absolute best. You need to be around those who challenge you and help you grow. Spend time with positive people who will inspire and motivate you. Find people who are relatable.

Imagine what you want your life to be. Visualize your future and then create it. In this particular case, you want a new career path. In order to do that, connect with people who are already established in that career who can give you guidance and insight. You need to be around people who will be honest, helpful, and give you feedback. You want those people to help steady you on the upcoming stepping-stones.

If you want to work from home, look for remote positions. If you want flexibility, seek freelance opportunities. If you want to make a six-figure salary, explore those opportunities. And then connect with those who can help you break into the field and navigate your career path.

When you are not networking, you can find other ways to level up by seeking more available resources. You can listen to podcasts that inspire you, read books and articles that make you think, watch shows that stir emotion, observe others who influence and motivate, and volunteer to provoke emotion.

Leveling up takes time. But by planting the seed, you can determine what you need to do to get there.

Surround yourself with the type of person you want to be. Think about who you spend the most time with. Is your "circle" pushing you forward or holding you back?

Beyond the Bell Bonus Tip:
Be aggressive and create the life you want.

I'M JUST A TEACHER

Never forget how wildly capable you are.

~Unknown

Know your worth, then add tax.

~Unknown

Opportunity is always knocking. The problem is that most people have the self-doubt station in their head turned up way too loud to hear it.

~Brian Vaszily

It's not who you are that holds you back, it's who you think you're not.

~Denis Waitley

"I'm just a teacher." How many times have you heard that? Or maybe you just thought it about yourself? Does your job constantly have you feeling like you don't have the right skills, or you feel inadequate? Does it cause you to have low self-esteem? Have you ever felt like a fraud? Do you feel like you don't belong or don't feel as intelligent or qualified as you really are? If so, you have fallen into the trap of imposter syndrome. It's a term that describes how people fail to recognize their own success and accomplishments.

Imposter syndrome is real. It is a roadblock to keep you from moving forward. It can be detrimental to you as you wrap up your teaching career, and as you are deciding what to do to get out and find a new career path.

I fell into this snare as I was considering my next step. I was losing myself and who I was and what I was truly skilled and qualified to do. I felt inadequate and thought I couldn't find anything else to do because teaching was all I knew. Many times, I felt like being a teacher was my only identity. It was who I was and what I did.

Don't fall into this trap! Don't believe this lie! You are so much more than "just a teacher." What I failed to realize is that teachers have so many transferable skills. Teachers are so much more skilled than they give themselves credit for.

Look at what you have done as an educator. Think about all the lives you've changed. On any given day, teachers answer more than 1,500 questions and make more decisions than a brain surgeon.

Teachers are amazing! We are courageous. We are advocates. We inspire and transform lives. Yes, we are teachers ... but we are so much more! Take credit for your abilities and know your worth!

Beyond the Bell Bonus Tip:

You are more than just a teacher!

NETWORK, NETWORK, NETWORK

Everyone you will ever meet knows something you don't.

~Bill Nye

*The richest people in the world look for and build networks.
Everyone else looks for work.*

~Robert Kiyosaki

Networking was a key factor for me in getting out of the classroom! I cannot stress enough the importance of networking!

Networking does not come completely natural to me. Therefore, this was something I had to work on, and really make a conscious effort to put myself out there. It was definitely a learning curve because you don't know what you don't know. But the return on my effort has been huge! This has truly been one of the biggest game changers.

By networking, you are essentially joining a community. But in order to make the most of it, you need to be active, and you can't be afraid to ask for help. Put away your pride and look at it as a way you are investing your time and energy into yourself. Get ready to reach out to people who you don't even know and send emails to complete strangers.

The first step I personally took was that I made a list of friends and family in my life who I felt could help me. I reached out to those people via emails, texts, and phone calls and told them my situation and what I was looking to do and asked if they had any ideas or suggestions. From doing this, I ended up reconnecting with a childhood friend I hadn't seen in over 20 years! He supported me and gave me the contact information for a job recruiter. This also led to me reconnecting with a family member I hadn't seen in a while, and he became a constant prayer partner during this time of transition.

After this, I set up a LinkedIn profile. LinkedIn is like Facebook for businesses. I didn't have one at all when I started looking at a career change because I didn't know I needed one. I created a profile around October, and by the end of the month, I only had about 23 connections. Of those connections, only about three of those were people who I actually knew or lived locally; the rest were complete strangers. The more I was on there, the more connections I made. I knew I needed to grow my network, so on the many occasions I reached my weekly limit of connections, I would have to wait until the following week to add anymore contacts. It grew quickly and by January, I had over 1,000 connections. LinkedIn will become your new best friend.

Once you decide the route you want to go in, I recommend changing your LinkedIn title. For example, I changed my LinkedIn profile from elementary school teacher to Future Instructional Designer six months before I resigned. Be sure to also change your profile to say "open to work." This way, when people, connections, and recruiters view your profile, they know you are looking for a job and also what line of work you are interested in pursuing.

My next suggestion would be to join as many social media groups as possible that are geared toward what stage you are in and what field you are looking to break into. For example, I joined groups that were geared specifically to helping teachers get out of teaching, and also Instructional Design groups because that was what I wanted to do. I cannot tell you how helpful these groups are at helping you when you get discouraged and for cheering you on. Surround yourself with people who push you, challenge you, and help you grow. Be around people who are like-minded and who have achieved the ultimate goal you want.

This community I was now a part of was (and still am) had some of the nicest, most helpful, talented, and incredibly genuine and caring people I have ever met. I received more positivity from these complete strangers than I did from people I actually knew. They were more than willing to help or show support in any way possible. They offered to get on Zoom meets, or call me, or chat to answer questions I had or offered to be an accountability partner, or give free consultations. People contacted me about collaborating on projects or asking if I needed a mentor. Some were emailing me to share some positivity in my job search, or to share job openings, or tagging me in posts with upcoming webinars and workshops. Others would suggest other people to follow and give me book recommendations or recommendations for e-learning courses and classes. I received messages of encouragement and people telling me how impressed they were with the skills I had on my profile. They told me people to follow on LinkedIn, what websites to use to look for jobs, articles to read, and books to buy. They gave me so much information. I received so much support from people I didn't even know. I reached out to people asking if a company they just got hired at had any more open positions, or if they had any other suggestions of things I needed to be doing. I also suggest reaching out and making connections with specific people from the company where you are trying to get a job. I had virtual meetings with people from not only across the country, but also on the other side of the world!

Networking on social media caused a domino effect. My two mentors and my job trainer who helped me, were also from connections. I met one of my mentors, Leena, on a social media site. After responding back and forth to a few posts, we started messaging each other, which led to a Zoom meet, which later led to emails, phone calls and texting. She had helped other teachers get through the hurdle of leaving the classroom, as she was a classroom teacher herself, and knew what to do to get out. I was thankful because now I was also going to receive her support. I told her I was looking to go into Instructional Design, and she shared other contacts to talk with who were more experienced in the field I was interested in. She also suggested a class to help me get prepared for career readiness. We have developed a relationship that may possibly lead to a future business venture! Our connection also led me to meet my trainer, Kathy, who met with me and told me she wasn't going to leave me, and she was going to stick with me to the end. My second mentor, Erica, came from a connection who suggested a particular learning platform. She ended up being one of my instructors. When that course was over, I reached out to her personally with some questions about leaving the classroom, as she was also a former teacher. She offered to meet with me weekly. I will never forget her telling me, "Let's get you a job!" I am incredibly honored and privileged that these wonderful women stood by me during this time of my life. And I am grateful to call them my friends.

Another domino effect from networking led to some work opportunities. Two of the contractor positions I currently have are from connections I made, rather than from the over 400 applications and resumes I sent in. One was from one of my mentors, who posted a freelance position for a company where I am writing educational case studies. Another position was from taking a class. In this particular class, we were divided into groups for assignments. When this class ended, four of us from our group joined together, and we are now working under the business name from one of the women in that group designing courses.

My third tip would be to utilize YouTube blogs, podcasts, and industry-related articles. For example, I read articles that mentioned a person's name, so I would find that person and connect with them. I also listened to podcasts and connected with the guest speakers. I reached out to a guest speaker on social media and asked her to put me on her prayer list. Many times, someone posted a free course or webinar, and then I connected with the person presenting the course. And usually they had more courses, so I gained more education, certificates, and even more connections!

Do not underestimate networking and making connections! Who knows, starting a conversation with a complete stranger may create a new relationship. And that relationship could lead to a connection. And that connection may lead to a new career.

Beyond the Bell Bonus Tip:

Do not turn to the next page until you set up a LinkedIn profile and connect with at least 50 people.

Find a Mentor

We rise by lifting others.

~Robert Ingersoll

Colleagues are a wonderful thing—but mentors, that's where the real work gets done.

~Junot Diaz

I get by with a little help from my friends.

~John Lennon and Paul McCartney

If at all possible, find a mentor during this process. Mentors provide so much guidance, motivation, and emotional support during this transition. They help with exploring career options, goal-setting, and they can introduce you to resources and contacts.

I was fortunate to not only have one mentor, but I had two! I met my first mentor, Leena, in a social media group. We responded back and forth to a post. She was a classroom teacher and had helped other teachers transition out of the classroom. We started emailing, and then had phone conversations and video chats. She sent little messages of encouragement, or messages that said, "You will do great today," when she knew I had an interview. She introduced me to Kathy, who was a trainer at a college who helped get people ready for jobs and taught a job skills class. I met with Kathy on numerous occasions. Leena also helped with resources, connections, and my resume. She also told me where to look for classes to upskill.

My second mentor, Erica, was actually an instructor of mine in a cohort class I was taking to upskill. I reached out to her after the class and asked questions because she was a former teacher who transitioned into Instructional Design, which was the field I was trying to break in to. She offered to have weekly meetings with me. She gave me her personal number and told me to call anytime. Each week, either on the phone or video chat, we met to talk about the latest updates and challenges to my job search.

I cannot say enough about the wonderful women who stuck by me to the end. They were so helpful and supportive. They helped guide me and encourage me. They let me chat and text and ask questions. They were always "on call" when I needed them. I am so thankful for them and grateful they will always be friends. I hope that I will one day be able to give the support they gave to me, to someone else.

Try looking on social media pages, and in groups. Try to join as many groups as you can that are related to your goals and what you are trying to achieve. Another good place to look is LinkedIn, especially after you have made a lot of connections. I even had more than one person on LinkedIn who reached out to me and asked if I needed a mentor! Reach out to people and simply ask—you might be surprised at what they might say!

Until you find a mentor, look for an accountability partner. Find someone in a similar situation and wanting to transition as well. Or find someone that you know will hold your feet to the fire until you reach your goals. The point is, just find someone to keep you on track until you find a mentor.

Beyond the Bell Bonus Tip:

Try to find a mentor or an accountability partner this week.

LEARN

I will forever consider myself to be a lifelong learner. So, I thought of this as a season of growing, exploring, and acquiring new skills.

Once you have decided what direction you want to go in, you may need to fill in the knowledge gaps. Take this time to learn a new skill set. Now is the time to hone your best skills and interests.

In my situation, I knew there was a gap in what I knew and had been doing for years, and the direction I wanted to go to reach my end goal. So once again, I became a student, and like a sponge, I soaked up as much knowledge as I possibly could. I tried to absorb every piece of information that I could get a hold of. This was not only academically, but also trying to figure out how the "corporate" world was going to work. I learned that most hiring managers are looking for experience more than a degree. And I also knew that companies that were interested in me would see my hard work and initiative to upskill and bridge the gap.

I immersed myself in knowledge and information. I don't think I have ever learned so much in such a short amount of time. I listened to podcasts, watched webinars, read e-books, ordered books from my local library, and purchased books from Amazon. I downloaded free resources, bookmarked helpful sites, signed up for free workshops, and watched YouTube videos. At one time, I had signed up for 12 classes at the same time! I was taking online classes, reading articles, and learning strategies for today's jobs. I was continuing to learn with professional development, e-learning, mini online boot camps in the field I was interested in, and joining Zoom breakout rooms. I joined cohorts and signed up for free newsletters. I took four classes back-to-back. I went to live classes, had individual assignments, and team assignments. After I completed a class, earned a certificate, or learned a new still, I immediately added it to my resume, portfolio, and LinkedIn profile.

I was so busy. It felt like I had another full-time job! Despite being exhausted, I felt accomplished at the end of the day because I had done something to help my future. By the end of March, classes were winding down and my life was starting to get somewhat back to normal.

By completing classes and getting recognition, I boosted my confidence. I was receiving certificates and finishing projects. I felt so accomplished. I was receiving everything that I was lacking from my teaching job.

In addition to upskilling and improving your hard skills, you also need to develop your character and soft skills. Work on being a better person, a better you. Spend some time reflecting on yourself and the qualities you possess. What parts about you are going well? Where could you grow? What are you learning today to change your future?

Beyond the Bell Bonus Tip:
Never stop learning!

TRANSFERABLE SKILLS

The number one skill in life is not giving up.

~Bryant McGill

Every skill you acquire doubles your odds of success.

~Scott Adams

Most teachers are unaware of their abilities, talents, and proficiencies. They are either too modest, or have been overlooked, or placed in the category of a glorified babysitter for so long they feel inadequate. Teachers don't give themselves enough credit for the skills that they do have and what they bring to the table. They fail to realize their expertise and experience can be translated into a new role.

When you are making the transition from teaching, you will need to identify what those skills are, and how they are going to impact your new career and impress your future employer. Because you do have adaptable and desirable skills!

I do believe many companies hire the person for the job based on the right attitude, because skills can always be taught. But with that being said, I think it is a good idea to recognize the equipment in your toolbox.

Teachers have a lot to offer because they are lifelong learners. They are also continuously going through professional development.

In my situation, I needed to make sure my skills sounded more tech focused. I had to make sure the wording was transferred into the field I was pursuing. I had to make sure it would translate into the corporate setting.

Think about the duties you perform every day. Even if you have only taught for a few years, you have acquired certain traits that are highly marketable. Keep a list of these skills close by for future reference. Some of them may include:

Interpersonal, public speaking, coaching, mentoring, training, supervising, leadership, persuasion, negotiating, mediation, customer service, logical thinking, problem-solving, creative thinking, decision-making, planning, organization, writing, research, technological, performing, adaptability, perceptual, project management, presentation, coordination, implementation, content development, managing, negotiating, lesson planning, time keeping, data entry, leadership development, breaking down complex concepts

The list goes on and on. Feel free to use this list. Think about other duties and responsibilities that are transferable skills and add to it. Have confidence in your abilities and in what you have to offer.

Beyond the Bell Bonus Tip:
You have incredible transferable skills!

UPDATE YOUR RESUME

If you're unhappy in your job, one small decision you can make today is updating your resume. That's the first, and very important step, in starting the job search process.

~Ken Coleman

I cringed at the idea of having to make, well, I should say remake, a resume. But I knew I had to do it. I really didn't know where to start. I hadn't made a resume in 18 years!

I looked through my saved documents on my computer and found a rough sketch of one I had started a few years ago when I was considering leaving education. I took the information from it and started adding to it and making updates.

Then I began doing some research and seeing what jobs today were looking for in a resume. I bought a pretty resume template from Etsy and started plugging in my professional information, an updated photo, and recent skills to create a newer one.

Then when I took a course on what I was trying to change careers to, it had a resume template, so I created another one that was geared more toward Instructional Design.

I think by summer I had created a total of about five or six resumes, but it didn't just stop there. I was constantly tweaking and revamping my resume as I learned new skills and gained experience.

Teachers have many relevant skills for careers outside the classroom. They just need a bit of help adapting their resume to convey those skills to a potential employer.

Something very important that I learned was to stay away from saying too much about teaching and being in the classroom because that is not the field I was trying to get a job in. That's hard to do when that's the only thing I'd done for nearly two decades!

Here are some tips for writing a resume using your teaching skills in a new career:

1. Include your teaching experience, but do not begin your resume with it
2. Instead of saying teaching, mention your experiences such as curriculum design and collaboration
3. Use verbs such as curated, created, designed, developed, measured, adapted, researched, implemented
4. Include tech tools you have used and also ones you are proficient in such as Word, Excel, PowerPoint, etc.
5. Instead of focusing so much on teaching, point out how you developed lesson plans and curriculum to meet objectives
6. Emphasize your writing skills
7. Include how the objectives you wrote were assessed
8. Note how you aligned instruction to meet objectives
9. Consider adding a numerical value of something your student accomplished such as a percentage of gain from the beginning of the year to the end
10. Include any adapted instruction to meet diverse learners

Some important key tricks to getting your resume noticed are:

1. Include soft skills
2. Tailor your resume with specific skills for the role you are seeking
3. Continuously update
4. Share it on LinkedIn
5. Have several resumes readily available that you could send depending on the role you are seeking

Creating an updated resume is a lot of work! It is time-consuming, and you will probably go through several drafts. Remember, this is your time to shine and show what you can do. Add your key skills, significant accomplishments, and best attributes. Ask yourself: What do I have to offer?

Beyond the Bell Bonus Tip:

This is not a time to be modest!

CREATE A PORTFOLIO

A career is a portfolio of projects that teach you new skills, gain you new expertise, develop new capabilities, grow your colleague set, and constantly reinvent you as a brand.

~Tom Peters

I'm looking to expand my portfolio while I'm on top and while I'm young.

~Floyd Mayweather Jr.

When you are applying for jobs, it is not only industry standard to have a portfolio, but it is expected. You will need to create a digital portfolio to showcase your abilities. So, let's talk a little bit about what they are, what they should include, and why you need one.

A portfolio is a visual and digital representation of your work. It is basically an extension of your resume. Your resume tells what you can do, but your portfolio shows it. A lot of times resumes alone are not strong enough to break you into a new career path or get the job. The benefit of having a portfolio is that it shows the skills and versatility that are not necessarily showcased on your resume.

Portfolios tell a story … your story. It is your personal journey. A portfolio shows your creativity and range of the types of work you can do. It is like a digital diary that shows your personal growth and development, where others can see your progression of work.

A portfolio is a sales tool. It shows your potential and serves as a marketing tool for you. It gives you the opportunity to highlight your skills and what you can do, what you are proud of, and what you want to show.

The best portfolio pieces come from actual experience. If you are looking for ways to get experience, try volunteering or an intern position.

You may also try being someone's assistant or by doing some freelance work.

If you want to get started on a project but are having trouble coming up with ideas, try godesignsomething.co for inspiration. This site will help you get started.

When designing your portfolio, there are several important things you need to consider. What is your purpose for creating this portfolio? What is this portfolio going to achieve? What can you provide for the company? Having a clear answer to these questions will help you better develop your portfolio.

You will need to select a platform to house your portfolio. It could be as simple as PowerPoint slides. I know of many people who use Google Sites or other free websites. Any of these are acceptable because it gives you something to refer to in the interviewing process. If you struggle with designing, use a template or something that is pre-built so that it looks professional and leaves a great impression.

I would break the portfolio into at least four different sections. You will want to include an About Me section where you have your name, picture, contact information including your email, LinkedIn profile, and phone number. I would have another section of your skills and education. You will want to put anything related to the job you want and examples of the type of work you want to do. I would include another section that includes your mission and purpose. And lastly you will need to include projects. They need to demonstrate your ability to solve a problem and that you can work with different types of media.

It really helps to know what field you want to go into so that you can streamline your work samples in your portfolio. In my portfolio, because I wanted to go into Instructional Design, I put samples of storyboarding, facilitator and participant guides, e-learning authoring tools, and video recording and editing tools. I wanted hiring managers to see that I knew how to work with different tools related to the industry. It proves that I can do what I say I can do.

Some ideas to include in your portfolio are photos, writing samples, video, voiceover, audio, art, and design. You could also add lessons, online activities, e-learning, training videos, and tutorials. You'll just want to make sure it looks clean, attractive, professional, and that it presents well to a hiring manager.

When your portfolio is complete, make sure you share it on LinkedIn so recruiters and hiring managers can see it. Also, include a link to it on your resume.

Portfolios are a ton of work and take a lot of time. Get started creating yours and make sure it shows what sets you apart from the rest of the applicants.

Beyond the Bell Bonus Tip:

Show what you can do!

JOB SEARCHING

Don't let fear and doubt tell you that your dream job doesn't exist or that you can't do it! Fear and doubt are liars that keep us from doing what we were created to do.

~Ken Coleman

How many of you have thought to yourself, *I'm still trying to figure out what I want to be when I grow up?* If you have, you are not alone. There are so many options out there, which is why I want to share with you what I did that escalated my job search.

When you decide on what you want to do and focus in on what direction you want to take, then these steps will help you find job opportunities. My job search may have taken me longer because I had no clue as to what I was going to do. I spent quite a bit of time in the "exploring" phase, which is completely fine, but it just took me a bit longer before I started applying to jobs specifically in the field I was determined to break into.

Job searching is exhausting! It is time-consuming and frustrating. For me, searching for a full-time job felt like a full-time job. I recall watching an episode of Dr. Phil years ago and remembering him saying that if you don't have a job, you need to spend the time you would be working at that job, actually looking for a job. Well, I can honestly say I think Dr. Phil would be pleased with me.

Job searching was hard at first because I felt like my self-esteem and confidence had taken such a blow in the environment where I had been for so long. And I felt like I was "just a teacher" and didn't know what else I could possibly do but teach.

I felt like a fish out of water. I hadn't applied to jobs in almost two decades. I had been in the education bubble and had no idea other careers for teachers even existed. I felt boxed in and didn't think there was anything out there for me. But with a lot of hard work and determination, I changed my mindset.

When I first began job searching for Instructional Design positions, my focus was not solely about income. As we all know, teachers don't make that much anyway. I wanted to find something where I had a better work-life balance and a career where I was treated with respect and as an adult, and where I hopefully didn't have to take a pay cut. I discovered there are so many jobs and career paths that I am qualified to do that offer a much better heath and financial package.

One of the first steps I took was that I changed my LinkedIn profile to say Future Instructional Designer. I wanted all of my connections to know that I was an aspiring ID trying to find a career in that field. Then I changed my profile picture banner on LinkedIn to "open to work" so that connections and recruiters would know I was looking for a job.

Next, I set up job alerts. These were with LinkedIn, Glassdoor, Indeed, Edsurge, etc. (I have included a section at the end of the book for job search resources). I had all sorts of job boards sending me emails. Some were daily, some were once a week, or several times a week, and others were multiple times a day. Some companies were even sending me text alerts to my phone. I literally had hundreds of job alerts coming to me each day. I spent hours and hours browsing round the clock. I knew I was going to make a career transition, but before I did, I had a lot of jobs to sift through.

Some ideas for job titles to search for or put alerts in for are:

Digital learning, instructional designer, instructor led training, curriculum developer, trainer, learning and development, training and development, learning experience designer, e-learning, technical training, learning management

Don't be surprised if after you have made connections and joined social media groups, you will probably get recruiters reaching out to you by phone or email because they saw your profile or resume. And don't be afraid to reach out to them as well. I reached out quite a few times to hiring managers and talent acquisition at companies I had an interest in working for.

It was very labor intensive, but I knew it was temporary. It was also energizing and motivating at the same time because I knew with all of my hard work, I wouldn't be in the same position a year from now. I knew with each job that came along, I was one step closer to my goal. It was a simple reminder of where I was headed.

Beyond the Bell Bonus Tip:
Make Dr. Phil proud!

APPLY

The results you achieve will be in direct proportion to the effort you apply.

~Denis Waitley

You miss 100 percent of the shots you don't take.

~Wayne Gretzky

Word of warning, you need to grow some pretty thick skin before you begin applying to jobs. More than likely, you will be rejected, so just go ahead and get used to the idea—just don't take it personally.

I applied to over 60 jobs before I decided on what I really wanted to do and go into. I applied to anything from part-time, full-time, seasonal, and contract work. I sent applications for sales rep positions, medical device sales, and textbook companies. I sent resumes to companies that didn't even have job postings, and to places that didn't have any available positions I was seeking, just in case something else were to come open in the future, and I wanted them to know I would be interested in working for their company. Some jobs I heard back from multiple times, some were "no's," some that said the position was already filled or the position was no longer available, and some I never heard from ever again. I never knew there were so many different ways of companies saying "no" or telling you they would not proceed any further with your application. I had so many I think I could write a book just on their responses.

At the beginning of my search, I kept saying to myself that if I can only get a job by the time I get out of school for summer break, where I would hopefully not take a pay cut, then I would be happy. But as time went on, I knew I was short changing myself. There were a lot of jobs out there and I needed to ask for more. So I became choosier and looked for jobs that offered way more than what I was getting at my current job.

Once I knew the direction I wanted to go into, it made it much easier because I was focused on those positions or something very similar to it, instead of just applying like a shot in the dark. I kept track of the dates I applied, company names, and the position title, in a notebook. I had so many, that I had to refer back to my notebook to see if I had already applied to that position!

By May, I had put in over 300 applications, and by the end of June it was over 400. I had applied to so many that it didn't bother me that I got a rejection letter. It just meant that wasn't the job for me and something else better was out there for me.

My advice is even if you get rejected, and you will, try not to take it personally. Just keep applying, even if you don't meet all the criteria. Take a chance and apply anyway. Most companies are more interested in your abilities in what you can do, than your actual education and degrees. Yes, degrees do help, but ultimately it comes down to how you can contribute to the company. They want to know what you can do for them and how you fit into their culture.

Before submitting your applications, I recommend using Jobscan. It is a tool that is built from algorithms in ATS, which stands for applicant tracking system. Jobscan reviews your resume and makes suggestions for improvement before you submit an application based on the job description.

Your goal is for your resume to get through the ATS. Its job is to sift and sort through thousands of applications. Most applications are never even looked at by a human. Typically, when you apply for a job online, your resume is first being processed by the ATS. This is why it is so important to have your resume updated with work experience, top skills, and qualifications, because you want to get your resume past the system and into the hands of an actual person.

Some tips for how to beat the ATS are:

- ◉ Tailor your resume to the job description
- ◉ Match your resume keywords so that they are relevant to the job description
- ◉ Don't use tables or columns
- ◉ Save your file as a .docx

Sometimes you will find an open position that sounds like your "dream job," and it is so tempting to apply for that job and then stop applying to any others because you just know that this is the one! But do not fall into this trap. Do not put all of your eggs into one basket. In the corporate world, sometimes it takes weeks to hear back from an application, if you even do hear back. If you don't get your "dream job," you have lost weeks of applying to other potential positions.

Beyond the Bell Bonus Tip:

Keep applying until you sign a contract!

THE INTERVIEW PROCESS

In every success story, you will find someone who has made a
courageous decision.

~Peter F. Drucker

Say no to the demands of the world. Say yes to the longings of
your own heart.

~Jonathan Lockwood Huie

When I first started this process, the thought of interviewing was nerve-racking. I hadn't interviewed in over 18 years! But I remember a friend telling me that an interview is "just a conversation," and that seemed to help me put it in perspective.

I went through almost 50 interviews! I got so excited when I got a text or email from a recruiter of a company that wanted an interview or said, "your resume is impressive." It made me feel wanted and that people were interested in me.

For me, interviews were either feast or famine. It was like they came in waves. I would hear back from many companies all at once, and then it might be a ghost town for a couple of weeks. The biggest advice I can give during this silence is to keep being persistent.

From my personal experience, the interview process can take many forms. Take as many interviews as you can because if nothing else, you gain experience and, in turn, that increases your confidence. Interviews are good practice.

I want to share with you some examples of types of interviews I had, so you can get an idea of what yours could look like. There is a wide array depending on the company and where you apply. Here is just a sampling of some of the interview scenarios I went through:

- **Phone call interviews:** (Many happened this way for the initial interview.) I do recall one of these from Singapore at 6:00 in the morning. This was by far the earliest interview I've ever had. For those who may not know, sometimes you have to get through the recruiter before you are asked to go to the next round. Typically, it is like a screener call or meeting before the other interviews are scheduled. They want to get that initial impression of you before moving you on to the next stage. I also remember having a phone interview with HR and then the next week had an interview with the lead learning and development employee.

- **Email interview questions:** (The company wanted me to answer questions in written form before they were willing to take time for a phone call or meeting.) Then for some, the second step was for me to create a video for them telling them about myself, why I wanted the position, and also an example of me teaching and facilitating adults.

- **Self-recorded video interviews:** (This is where the questions popped up on the screen and then I would hit the start button and it would record me answering them.) I had about 30 seconds to read the question and then the recording would begin. You typically have three to four attempts to record and rerecord if you weren't happy with your answer or how you answered. I had multiple interviews of this type. One company wanted me to do a digital interview talking about myself and then answer three questions in 200 words or less.

- **Panel interviews:** (Also known as a "team" interview.) In this type of interview, be prepared for interviewees to take turns in round-robin questions.

- **Task interviews:** (This is when a company wants you to complete a project or show them something you can do.) One company wanted me to create a one-hour technical session to be implemented. I felt like they just wanted free work done. I felt uneasy about it, so I declined. A different company sent me an exercise to complete where I had to manipulate columns in the Excel program.

- **Automated audio interviews:** (I only recall one of these types of interviews.) This particular company was in Australia, and I had to call into a phone number. They asked questions and recorded my response. It was like leaving a voicemail, so you didn't actually get to speak to a real person.
- **Virtual job tryout interviews:** (This is where it was all on the computer and I answered a lot of questions.) Some were scenario based. They were trying to see how I would respond in situations and also how I worked best.

Beyond the Bell Bonus Tip:

Be prepared! You never know what type of interview you may get presented with.

CLEAN OUT YOUR ROOM

Clutter is the enemy of clarity.

~Julia Cameron

To put your things in order means to put your past in order, too.

~Marie Kondo

You can't reach for anything new if your hands are full of yesterday's clutter.

~Louise Smith

I began taking items from my classroom home in December. It was a tangible way of telling myself I'm really going to do this. I'm going to regain respect for myself, and I am going to leave education for good.

I was very discreet about the whole thing. I didn't want anyone to know what I was doing. I took about five to 10 things home each day. Most of them were books I had purchased, personal items, or picture frames, or anything fairly small that I could place in my tote bag. Items I knew I could get down the hall, out the door, and into my car without someone noticing or questioning what I was carrying home.

Each day I unloaded the car and made a neat stack downstairs in my house of years and years of teacher resources. Piles formed very quickly. It was a constant reminder that this was my final year, and I would be out of there by the end of May.

When my admin called me into the office in April and told me they were moving me to another school the next year, I really got to clean out my room. Everyone just thought it was because I would be teaching in another school and grade level. They had no idea I was cleaning everything out because I was about to leave the profession.

I gave a lot of things away to colleagues, friends, and people I had worked with in the past. I tried to get rid of as much as possible, so I didn't have to move it, store it, or take it home.

I also donated some items to a local thrift store. I sold some items to a new teacher who was just beginning her career. I sold faculty T-shirts and just about anything else I could find with the school logo on it. Quite a few teacher books I was able to sell on Amazon, but I also sold some items on social media sites. I sold my classroom library of books, and it went to another teacher from a nearby town. She was tickled pink, which made me feel good, knowing that she was going to use those books to further students.

Beyond the Bell Bonus Tip:
Get rid of what is standing in your way.

DO YOUR HOMEWORK

Listen to your gut, if it's telling you to quit, make the jump and quit. Just make sure to have a follow-up plan.

~Unknown

Before you resign, do your homework. Make sure you have a plan. Figure out your next move. Try to always be one step ahead of the game.

Questions if you are leaving your contract early:

- Will I be penalized?
- Will there be repercussions?
- Will I be fined?
- Is it considered abandonment of contract?
- Will anything go on my teaching certification?

Tasks to do before you turn in your computer:

- Save all of your files, emails, and documents
- Delete any browsing history, saved passwords, and files saved on your school computer
- Forward any emails you want to keep to your personal email and delete the rest

Insurance and retirement questions to ask:

- How will this change affect my retirement?
- Do I have vacation and personal days I need to take?
- Check on your retirement contributions or 401(k). Do you want to roll it over to an IRA?
- Figure out your budget—will you be making less? More? The same?
- When will insurance benefits end?

Try to use health insurance benefits and schedule doctor and dentist appointments before you leave. Sometimes it takes some time for a new insurance plan to begin with a new career. I left in mid-August and I had insurance until the end of October. I was offered COBRA as a continuation, but I worked it out where the insurance from my job kicked in on the day after my school insurance was over, so I did not have a gap.

Other questions to think about:

- ⊙ What day are you going to leave?
- ⊙ When are you going to tell your boss?
- ⊙ When are you going to tell your colleagues?
- ⊙ When will you submit your formal resignation?

Beyond the Bell Bonus Tip:

Make sure you have a solid plan in place.

SUMMER HUSTLE

Hustle in silence and let your success make the noise.

~Unknown

Contrary to popular opinion, the hustle is not a dance step—it's an old business procedure.

~Fran Lebowitz

Hustle until your haters ask if you're hiring.

~Unknown

I could not believe I survived another school year! I actually made it to the end. Now that it was summer, I could rest, be out of the classroom, and really focus on my next steps. I could breathe easier because I wasn't surrounded by a toxic work environment. I enjoyed my break and sense of freedom.

But I couldn't relax completely. I had about two months left to find a job! I was in full force mode applying and networking. I recall having four interviews in one day!

I was still applying to jobs and interviewing, but now I could really devote even more of my time to getting out of the classroom. It was like the final push.

Some days I was in panic mode because I knew I only had a couple of months to find something, or I would have to teach another year.

In June I revamped my resume … again. And tweaked my portfolio … again. And made sure my skills were front and center. Every day I was applying to jobs and connecting with people. By the end of June, I had over 2,000 connections and had applied to over 400 jobs!

In July, I made even more changes to my resume, and then turned my portfolio into a webpage. I realized that I will always be making changes to them as I further my career and learn new skills.

Beyond the Bell Bonus Tip:

As soon as you learn something new, add it to your resume and portfolio!

DON'T PANIC

You don't have to control your thoughts. You have to stop letting them control you.

~Dan Millman

Don't Panic? Yeah, right! Sometimes that's easier said than done. Especially if you are in need of a career change, but nothing seems to be panning out for you. I was about to start panicking when summer came, and then June passed, and July got here and still no job. I knew I had a month left to find something or I was going back to the classroom for another year. I'll tell you more about my story and what happened to me in a bit.

But in the meantime, if you find yourself still without a job and the school year is about to begin, or if you just need a way out right now and you have no other options, here are some things to consider.

- Could you find a "now" job and not your forever job for the time being?
- Do you have enough money saved up so you could leave or not return to the classroom while you still search for jobs?
- Do you have a partner who could temporarily support you financially?
- Do you have another business or source of income that could support you?
- Could you take a leave of absence?

- While you are still searching, here are some things you can do.

- Freelance—Companies look for freelancers all the time! This could be a great way to get experience with a variety of projects. This would help showcase your skills on your resume and portfolio. Freelance work can often lead to full-time work.

- ⊙ Reach out—I recommend reaching out to companies that you are interested in working for and see if you could do a small project for them. This foot in the door could lead to more projects with the company or even a full-time job.

A lot of companies want to fill positions around August for their fiscal year budget. Even if you have to teach a bit longer, I don't want you to feel like it will cause you to give up on your dreams of leaving the classroom.

Beyond the Bell Bonus Tip:

Remember, timing is everything.

How I Decided What to Do and What Direction I Chose to Go

Sometimes in the waves of change we find our true direction.

~Unknown

When I decided this would be my final year as a teacher, I did lots and lots of research. One of my favorite search questions was—what are other jobs that teachers do?

Instructional Design kept popping up. Everywhere! It was like the universe was saying: THIS IS YOUR SIGN.

I wasn't familiar with Instructional Designers, so I did some research and discovered that they apply methodology to design and develop content to support the acquisition of new knowledge. They conduct needs analysis to determine the needs of the learner (i.e., what the learner should know or be able to do as a result of the training). In simple terms, in a corporate setting, they analyze business needs and come up with learning solutions for those needs.

I discovered that teachers make great Instructional Designers because they have incredible transferable skills, knowledge, and experience from the classroom. Teachers and IDs share many of the same and similar qualities. Teachers have been using ID skills since entering the classroom, but they don't realize it. They understand the needs of learners and typically have strong analytical skills. They work with content and develop curriculum. Teachers also incorporate a variety of problem-solving and real-life scenarios into their assessments and knowledge checks. Plus, teachers have a lot of experience with time management, flexibility, and interpersonal skills.

Even though further education was not necessary, I realized there was a gap between teaching students and teaching adults. I needed to brush up on theories I had learned in college, and also theories I was not at all familiar with. I wanted to fill the gap while making this transition because I knew it would make me more marketable and also show my initiative.

So, once I decided this is what I wanted to go into, I started finding classes and seeing what was available. I took a class that was catered specifically to teachers getting into ID. Then I took another course to get me prepared for corporate ID. Then I signed up for a couple of other classes for e-learning. I believe these classes and cohorts gave me an edge in getting into the field.

Beyond the Bell Bonus Tip:

Once you decide what you want to do, be open to learning and growing.

MY INTERVIEW PROCESS

An interview is not a rearview mirror, it's a chance to drive the car forward.

~Emily Hawkins

I had several interviews in the fall, but the interviews really started picking up in February. It was such a great feeling, like I was going fishing by throwing my resume out there and then waiting for a "bite."

Recruiters were also reaching out to me for jobs I didn't even apply to. I felt wanted. Every interview I had was different. And each time I met with a company, or had a screener call, it built my confidence because it meant people were interested in me and what I had to offer.

As I am writing this, I am technically employed by three different companies. All three processes of getting these jobs were very different. I wanted to share those experiences with you.

In January, I took a class on ID. This was a cohort that met twice a week, and within the class, we were grouped into teams. My team was a group of women from all over the U.S. We named our group WWID (Wonder Women of Instructional Design). The class was intense. We had individual assignments, but also group assignments. Because of the workload and having to collaborate and work on projects, we met on a regular basis and were in constant communication through email and Slack. In March, four women including myself from this group, decided to join together, and we started working on a project for the "leader" of our team who already had an established company. This was a great opportunity because we already knew we could work well together, so this was a no-brainer! It was a great job opportunity, invaluable experience, working with some incredible women, and earning some extra money on the side creating courses.

Around April, one of my mentors had posted a job on social media, and I reached out to her and asked if it was something I could do. She ended up sending my resume to her company. It was for writing educational case studies. Shortly after, I had a phone interview with a supervisor from the company. We spoke on the phone twice for about 15 minutes, and then I had the job! It wasn't even like an interview. It was more about what my experience was and what they were looking for. He said he was impressed with my background and liked me. The phone conversation went so well that they ended up not only contracting me for the case studies writing position, but also for another position. Shortly after, I had another meeting with the same guy and also a meeting with the product manager. In mid-May, I signed a contract with them. So, this came from a connection, not a job application.

My third job, I applied to at the very end of June. Around mid-July, the recruiter called me. We discussed the role and my experience. We had a great conversation, and she wanted to move me to the next interview. About two weeks later, I virtually met with two people from the company, lasting about an hour. They said they were still doing interviews and would let me know soon. Well, the recruiter called me back the same day! I was shocked! I didn't expect to hear back so soon! She wanted to move me forward with the next two interviews. She wanted to do one of them the following Monday. I told her I would be happy to, but I had to go back to work that day, as my summer break was over, and I could schedule it after I got in from work. Instead, she worked me in and got the next one scheduled for the very next day, and the last interview, the day after that. I ended up having back-to-back-to-back interviews! The next day I had another team interview. It was supposed to be with three people but ended up being only two since one of them was having trouble with a flight getting home. It was for another hour. It went really well. After it was over, I prepped for my last interview, which was a presentation. The following day, I got up early to do last-minute prep work. I had to do a presentation about anything I wanted, but I needed to teach them something and make it interactive, so I chose photography. The interview was with four people, two of them were the same as my first-round interview, and two additional people. I gave my presentation, and they asked additional questions. I made sure I had done some research, so I was able to ask each one of them a question specifically catered to them and their experience. It went well and I felt confident. I was very transparent with what I was looking for a job and why. One of the women on the panel just thanked me for being an educator and what teachers had done throughout the pandemic. Another woman on the panel gave me kudos for noticing I needed to do something for myself and my well-being. After the interview, I sent each of them a thank you email.

I had three interviews with this company alone, not including the other companies I had interviewed with in the same week. I was tired, but proud of myself. I knew I had given it my best. And thankfully, my hard work paid off because they hired me!

Beyond the Bell Bonus Tip:
Be prepared and confident!

I Got Hired

*If you find something you're passionate about, Monday will be
your favorite day of the week.*

~Jan Almasy

A few days after my interviews, I had to go back to work at school
for preplanning. I dreaded it. I didn't want to go. I didn't want to
be there. My heart wasn't in it. But I had to. Sunday evening, I remember
trying to prepare myself for work Monday morning. I had picked out
something to wear, got my tote bag ready, and I went downstairs to go
through all the supplies I had taken home back in May. I recall thinking
to myself, "I can't go into work with nothing." I found a small, clear
container and put in the bare necessities, which included a pen, pencil,
dry erase marker, a roll of masking tape, and a stapler.

Monday morning, I went to work. I went to my new school and
talked with some of the teachers in my grade level. It was filled mainly
with meetings, and thankfully didn't have much time to do anything else.
After work, I went home and was preparing to take my mom out for her
birthday, when I got a phone call from the city where the company I had
interviewed with last week. I knew it was about the job. And I knew I
either had it or I didn't. It was my hiring manager. She was in two of the
interviews, and she called me directly. We took a few moments to make
small talk and then she said, "I have a question for you ..." and she offered
me the job! I think I nearly screamed into the phone! I was so excited!
And then my excitement caused my dog to start barking and carrying on.
We were all celebrating! I thanked her for calling and making it the best
day. I was so happy I was nearly in tears. Finally, after months and months
of hard work, I got the job!

120

Beyond the Bell Bonus Tip:

Your hard work will pay off!

I RESIGNED

*You know when you just have to walk away from things that
don't align with you anymore? Yeah, I just quit my job.*

~Dau Voire

*Today I close the door to the past, open the door to the future,
take a deep breath, step on through and start a new chapter in
my life.*

~Unknown

In late April, I signed my contract for the next year. I didn't want to, but I didn't have a full-time job lined up, so I didn't really have a choice. I had to have a job and at least by signing it, it gave me some security.

I received a phone call on Monday at the beginning of August from the hiring manager and asked if I wanted the job. On Tuesday, I received a verbal offer from the recruiter. On Thursday, the actual contract came through. It was surreal. I knew I had been preparing for this for months and it was finally here. It was hard to believe! I knew this was what I wanted, but I was still struggling with ending my teaching career and what I needed to do. The hiring manager sent me a text and told me that she knew it was a hard change and if I needed to call or text her anytime that I could, and that her team would always be her top priority. Well, that was all I needed to hear. It sealed the deal for me. I called her and I signed the contract while I was on the phone with her.

Shortly after signing the contract, I sent a very informal email to admin and HR that said I was resigning. I spoke with the principal briefly after he called me to come to his office. I printed out the email, signed it, and turned it in. I worked the rest of that week. On Sunday night, I sent a group text to the teachers in my grade level to let them know I had resigned. Then on Tuesday and Wednesday, I met with parents for "meet your teacher." It was so awkward telling them, "Welcome to second grade, but I'm not going to be your teacher this year." I had my first day of school with students on Thursday, and my last day of school on Friday. It was so strange getting a job on my first day back to school, signing a contract and resigning on the fourth day of school, and having my first day and last day with students in the same week!

On my last day of school, I will never forget it, the principal did not say a word to me. No one from the board of education or HR said anything to me. The only person who did was the assistant principal. She came up to me and wished me the best of luck and for me to turn in my keys, badge, and computer before I left. You would think that I would have gotten some sort of thank you for 18 years of service or we will miss you or something. There was nothing. They didn't care if I stayed or left. I have never felt so disposable in my life. It just validated everything I already knew. And this was why I needed to go.

Beyond the Bell Bonus Tip:

Have your resignation letter ready for when you sign your new contract!

WHAT I DO NOW

Don't be afraid to start over. This time you're not starting from scratch, you're starting from experience.

~Unknown

As you'll recall, I technically have three jobs. One is more freelance and the other one I will work on as we have projects. But the one I'm going to focus on in this chapter is the one I work full-time.

Do you remember a few chapters back when I got moved to another grade level because of my "skill set" yet no one told me what that was? I was belittled by the admin at my school and simply told that was where I was going to be placed. Turns out, my "skill set" was suited for something a little higher than second grade, and that is in a corporate environment

As I am writing this, I just finished my second month in my new career. While I had absolutely no experience in the insurance industry, I had skills and knowledge that allowed me to transition over into this field. I work in the learning and development department. I guess you could say that I wear a few different hats as far as job titles go. I'm a Learning Project Specialist. In this role, I work on various projects, design and deliver training, and use Instructional Design skills to analyze and devise interventions to close performance gaps. There is also a teaching component with this position, so I still get to teach! It seems to be the best combination for me!

My day-to-day varies, but consists of developing, designing, and writing training curriculum. I may implement, coordinate, or provide training in-house with associates. I am establishing learning objectives and determine training needs and deliver on those needs, which contribute to the success of personnel, so I am contributing to their professional growth.

WHAT MY LIFE LOOKS LIKE NOW

*If there's even a slight chance of getting something that will make
you happy, risk it. Life's too short, and happiness is too rare.*

~A.R. Lucas

My life has been completely flipped upside down—in a good way! I
never imagined I would have so many life changes in such a short
amount of time.

With this career change, I have a lot more breathing room. I have a
work-life balance. I can drink as much water as I want to because I can
actually go to the bathroom when I need to. I have time to actually chew
my lunch before swallowing. My workday is flexible, and I pretty much
get to set my own hours. I can go to town or run errands when I need to.
I wear shorts or yoga pants and sit on the porch or in a comfy chair every
day. I get to spend the entire day with my dog. I get to sleep in longer
and don't have to drive to work. I don't have to pack my lunch, grade
papers, organize field trips or parent involvement, make copies, enter
grades, or prepare for fire drills. If I need to step away to take a phone
call, I can. If I have a headache, I can stop working and come back to it
later. I don't have to worry about discipline problems, recess duty, or
making sure students got on the right bus to go home. I don't have to
worry about testing or have test pressure anymore. I can say what I want
on social media without being reprimanded, and I can be seen out in
public during the middle of the day. I don't have to wait until after school
to go to the grocery store. I do not have to make four-page lesson plans
when I need to be out. If I go to a doctor's appointment, I don't have to
worry about being "seen" if I decide to go shopping afterward. Instead
of being rewarded with a candy bar or a new lanyard, I get time off and
bonuses. I have more privacy. I have freedom and I am treated like an
adult. Every day I am learning, growing, and happy.

My life has gone through some major changes during the past few months. It's been like a whirlwind. But thankfully that whirlwind has taken me to a place I now get to call home.

HOW MY LIFE HAS CHANGED

I'm no longer accepting the things I cannot change.
I'm changing the things I cannot accept.

~Angela Davis

Since making the career change, my life has changed in so many ways. The only regret that I have is that I didn't make the change sooner. If I had only known how much better my life would be, I would have left years earlier. I truly wish I could bottle up how I am feeling and share it with each of you so you would be able to see how sweet life can be.

I am happier. My life is back in balance. I am not stressed, and I do not have anxiety. I enjoy going to work. I look forward to projects and what I contribute to the company. I no longer get the "Sunday night blues."

I love that I have flexibility and room for growth. I can leave work at work, close my computer and shut my work off at the end of the day.

I feel respected, valued, supported, and I'm treated like family. I am appreciated for my creativity and what I bring to the company. I appreciate my manager and I love the positive relationship I have with her and my team. I am reminded that I am working *with them*, not *for them*. I have high respect for the people above me. They want me to learn, grow, and be successful. They are kind, welcoming, and always willing to help. There are so many opportunities for advancement.

I thought I had reached my peak in my career or "working years," but I have a newfound hope. I am living my best life and thriving in this culture and climate.

The days are flying by. It's like the weekend gets here and I can't believe it's already here. I am not on the countdown for the next break or holiday. I actually feel like going and doing things after work ... and I have the energy to do so.

I knew when I was looking for a job, I wanted growth and opportunities. I wanted to continue learning. I wanted a culture I could thrive in, team members who supported me and wanted me to reach my goals and succeed. I wanted to be around people who were sincere and showed genuine concern for me as a member of not only their team, but as family. I wanted a place that would let me be creative and think outside the box. I wanted to be able to use the skills I had, but also expand and develop. I needed a company that was understanding of my transition and knew that I wouldn't know everything going into the position but was understanding of my situation. But I was questioning, is there really a job out there that could offer all of these things? Yes, there is. And the good news is, I'm just getting started!

PAY IT FORWARD

When you are lucky enough to be the recipient of an act of kindness, Please honor the giver by paying it forward.

~Unknown

You are not a true success unless you are helping others be successful.

~Jon Gordon

Beginning in January, I had people start reaching out to me for advice on leaving the classroom. People I didn't know and had never met. They knew I was a teacher and heard I was transitioning and wanting to know what steps to take to get going. They were sending me messages on social media and LinkedIn asking for help and suggestions on what I was doing.

I received so much help and support along the way, I was more than willing to help! I gave suggestions for possible different routes they could take. I told them about some classes that were offered that would help them break into different fields.

I offered to have virtual meetings with people who were struggling as well. I sent them connections, job postings, and links to podcasts or resources that could be helpful.

I reviewed resumes, assisted with application questions, and QA'd portfolio pieces. While they were waiting to hear back from interviews or recruiters, or next steps, I sent emails or notes of encouragement.

I'm not telling you this to give myself a pat on the back. I am merely asking you to be aware of how others help you during this time, and to simply return the favor.

Beyond the Bell Bonus Tip:

When you get where you are going, help someone else in need.

Biggest Takeaways

1. Be committed
2. You can do this
3. Give yourself credit for who you are and what you do
4. Believe in yourself and your abilities
5. You are more than just a teacher
6. Know that you deserve better
7. Build on the skills you already have
8. Take a chance
9. Have a growth mindset
10. Put yourself out there

FINAL THOUGHTS

One can only sit on the fence so long without hurting.

~Minh Tan

In the end, we only regret the chances we didn't take,
relationships we were afraid to have, and the decisions we waited
too long to make.

~Lewis Carroll

My question to you is—Are you still on the fence? Or are you ready to take the next step? Before taking the leap, spend careful thought really looking at your life and where you are right now. If you aren't happy, or the path you are on is not going to take you to your goals, then get out … sooner rather than later.

Take a lesson from me and don't let 18 years slip away like I did!

MY CHALLENGE TO YOU

Oh, child just do what you love because you'll never get this life again.

~Robin Schulz

You are the architect of your own future, so design your future with uncompromising sincerity.

~Debasish Mridha

If you are shaking your head at anything you have read or if any of this resonates with you, I encourage you to regain control of your dreams and future.

If you can learn to let go of the fear and security blanket and cross over to the other side, you will see there is life beyond the bell.

I can't make the decision for you. It is up to you to decide. Are you happy with your life right now? Will things be different or the same five years down the road? If you want to leave the classroom, you can. You just have to be committed to putting forth the time and effort it will take. And it is a lot! But the payoff is sweet! Ask yourself—How bad do I want it?

My challenge for you is to make a plan. Set attainable goals. Seek support from friends and family. And just do it!

Personal Note

There really is life after teaching, and I'm living it! I hope this book provided you with some clarity and motivated you to take the next step, whatever that direction is, or wherever it may lead. Please believe in yourself and your abilities. Remember, I am cheering you on! You've got this!

Take care, teacher friends!

Reach Out

If you have an interesting story about how you left the classroom, or if this book helped you in any way, please reach out to me. I would love to hear from you and how you made your transition. You can find me on Facebook, Instagram, and LinkedIn.

I would like to leave you with this final quote:

One life. Just one. Why aren't we running like we are on fire towards our wildest dreams?

~Unknown

Favorite Resources

In the next several pages, you will find lots of resources! Some of these are from personal use, and others came highly recommended. I hope you find this section super helpful.

Resignation Letter Template

Below is a sample resignation letter. I suggest that you email this letter to the principal, assistant principal and the head of HR. Also, you should put a signed hard copy in the U.S. mail to the principal at the school and one signed copy in the U.S. mail to the HR director at the central office address. Remember, you do not owe anyone an explanation for your decision to resign.

Date

Mr. John Doe, Principal
School
Address
City, State, ZIP

Dear Mr. Doe,

Thank you for the opportunity to have worked at (School) for the past (number) years. I have really enjoyed working with the students, faculty, and administration at (Name of School). After careful consideration, I have decided to resign from my teaching position. I would like for my last day with the school system to be (date) or the last day of the (year–year) school year. Thank you for understanding.

Sincerely,

Your Name

Cc: (Name of HR), Director of Human Resources
 School Name

Resignation Letter if You Have Already Signed a Contract

Below is a sample letter you would submit if you have already signed a contract to teach next year. I suggest that you email this letter to the principal, assistant principal, and the head of HR. Also, you would put a signed hard copy in the U.S. mail to the principal at the school and one signed copy in the U.S. mail to the HR director at the central office address.

Date

Mr. John Doe, Principal
School
Address
City, State, ZIP

Dear Mr. Doe,

Thank you for the opportunity to have worked at (School name) for the past (number) years. I have really enjoyed working with the students, faculty and administration at (Name of School). Recently, I signed a contract to teach again for the upcoming (year–year) school year. However, after careful consideration, I would request to be released from next year's contract. I would like for my last day with the school system to be (date) or the last day of the (year–year) school year.

If it is not possible to grant my request to be released from the (year–year) teaching contract, then please accept this as my letter of resignation effective at the end of the (year–year) school year.

Thank you for your assistance with this matter.

Sincerely,

Your Name

Cc: (Name of HR), Director of Human Resources
   School Name

Sample Letter to Get Admin Off Your Back

Sometimes teachers who find themselves teaching in a place where they are unhappy and/or they are in constant conflict with the principal or other administration, submit a letter that says they are resigning effective at the end of the school year. By letting them know you are planning on leaving, they sometimes have a tendency to "back off" knowing that you will not be back the next year.

I suggest emailing this to your principal and assistant principal. I would also print it out and sign in and make copies. Then send one to the head of Human Resources at the central office, and also place one in the principal and assistant principal's mailbox at school.

Date

Mr. John Doe, Principal
School
Address
City, State ZIP

Dear Mr. Doe,

Thank you for the opportunity to have worked in (Name of School) for the past (number) years. I have really enjoyed working with the students, faculty, and staff at our school. However, after careful consideration, I want to go ahead and submit this letter of resignation effective at the end of the (year–year) school year.

Please know that I will work diligently to follow all of your directions from now until the end of the school year. It is important for me to be an effective teacher and cooperative colleague. I wanted to let you know as soon as I made my decision, so that the school system would have ample time to locate a replacement teacher for my position. Thank you for your assistance with this matter. I am looking forward to a productive remainder of the school year.

Sincerely,
Your Name

Cc: xxxx, Assistant Superintendent Human Resources
 Name of School

Other Careers for Teachers

- Virtual Assistant
- Corporate Trainer
- Museum Director
- Private Tutor
- Content Developer
- Education Product Supplier
- Educational Editor
- Learning and Development Specialist
- Instructional Designer
- Curriculum Writer
- Training Coordinator
- Educational Toy Company Consultant
- Textbook Sales Representative
- Educational Consultant
- Training and Development Manager
- Adjunct Professor
- Educational Writer
- Test Scorer
- Blogger
- Professional Speaker
- Researcher
- Government Trainer
- Teacher Resource Creator
- Instructional Coach
- Standardized Test Developer
- Sales Representative for Educational Textbooks
- Educational Consultant
- Grant Writer
- Youth Director
- Event Planner
- Edtech

Cover Letter Template

I created a cover letter template that I used as a starting point when applying to jobs. I always made changes to it to align directly with the company and position that I was applying for.

Name

Contact: Phone # Email Address Full Address LinkedIn Profile

Education: Degree, School, Year of Completion

Skills: (You could put something like: Self-Motivated, Reliable, Efficient)

HUMAN RESOURCES
Company Name
City, State
Date

TO WHOM IT MAY CONCERN

I am applying for the _____position I saw posted on _____. I am able to start _____. I believe I have a lot to offer your company.

I am interested in this type of work because _____.
This company attracted me because_____.
I enjoy _____ that your company offers.
_____ and _____ are very appealing to me.

I feel like this would be a great fit for me because _____.

Thank you for taking time to consider me for this position. I look forward to hearing from you soon.

Your Name

Resume Template

I used a resume template and made adjustments to it as needed for the jobs I was applying to. Make sure you use keywords and language from the job description.

Name
Your Title
Link to your portfolio

Contact: Phone # Email Address Full Address LinkedIn Profile

Summary/Objective

- Tell what you do and the experience and certifications you have. Talk about how you are excited to bring your knowledge and expertise to this opportunity.
- Tell what type of job you are seeking (part-time, full-time, remote, etc.)
- Tell why you are interested in working for this company.
- Include another link to see samples of your work.

Professional Experience

- List your title, place of employment, years
- Tell your contributions and list your employable skills
- List other accomplishments
- List additional work experience

Key Skills (List technical skills (e.g., Camtasia, Google Suite and soft skills, such as self-motivated, reliable, efficient)

Education (list degree, college, year of completion)
Continuing Education (list courses and certificates)
Strengths and Proficiencies (e.g., curriculum development, strategic planning)
Additional Information and Skills (e.g., creative thinker, lifelong learner)

How to Prepare for an Interview

First and foremost, if you have been asked for an interview, congratulations! You should be excited and proud of yourself because your hard work of creating a resume and applying to jobs has paid off and someone has taken notice! Now it's time to get prepared and show them why you are the best fit for their company.

1. **Study the job description**—Pay close attention to keywords that are mentioned multiple times. It may be a good idea to bring those up in the interview. Be prepared to tell how you fit what they are looking for. Mention how you have already achieved those key responsibilities they are looking for.

2. **Research the company and their website**—Be as informed as you can about the company. Take initiative and research the company's history, products or services they offer, accomplishments or awards, and growth. Pay close attention to their mission and values. Mention how you align with their vision.

3. **Show up early**—It's best to be early in case of traffic or parking, if you have to drive to the office, or if you run into some technical issues if the interview is virtual. You don't need to be in a situation where you end up giving the panel an excuse for being late or something went wrong. Being early also gives you time to get settled and be calm for the interview, which is going to give a great first impression.

4. **Dress professionally**—When you go in for your interview, or if it is a virtual interview, you will want to dress professionally. You don't want to be overdressed or underdressed, just dressed for the role you are hoping to get. Some common tips are to make sure clothing is not too loose or too tight, not revealing, and ironed. Basically, just don't look like you rolled out of bed.

5. **Remove distractions**—Leave your phone in the car, or if you do take it in, make sure you turn it off or put it on silent, and leave it in your purse or briefcase. If you are interviewing virtually from your home, make sure you put away or leave the room of anything that might make noise (children, pets, phones, TV, etc.)

6. **Have your resume or portfolio handy**—Many times during the interview, the interviewer will ask questions from your portfolio or resume. They may want you to explain more work history or talk about a project you completed. Have them readily available whether you do an in-person or virtual interview.

7. **Be honest**—No matter the questions they may ask during the interview, always be honest. Always tell the truth, but that doesn't necessarily mean you have to share everything. Answer the question and let them ask any follow-up questions if necessary.

8. **Be yourself**—Many companies hire a person because even if that person is lacking skills, they know those skills can be taught. They want the right fit for their mission and culture. If you end up getting the job and you were fake during the interview, they are going to find out right away. Always be your authentic self.

9. **Be engaged**—Be completely present and engaged during the interview. You want to show them you are confident and prepared. Be polite, smile, use good manners, make eye contact, and have great posture. You want your body language to communicate to them that you are interested and approachable.

10. **Send a thank-you note**—Shortly after the interview, send a quick note or email to the people who you interviewed with. You will want to thank them for their time and let them know you enjoyed learning more about them and the company. And you are welcome to mention how you hope to soon become part of the company.

Beyond the Bell Bonus Tip:

The more prepared you are, the more your confidence will shine in the interview!

Common Interview Questions

1. Tell me about yourself.
2. Why are you looking for a new position?
3. Why do you want to work at this company?
4. Why should we hire you?
5. What is your greatest strength?
6. What is your greatest weakness?
7. How do you handle stress?
8. Tell me about a time you had a disagreement with someone at work and how you handled it?
9. Tell me about a time you handled a difficult situation.
10. What interests you about this role?
11. What are three adjectives your colleagues would describe you as?
12. What do you want to be remembered for?
13. Can you work independently?
14. How have you demonstrated successful collaboration?

Depending on the job title, you will more than likely have additional questions tailored to that specific role. Some examples could be:

1. Have you designed curriculum?
2. How do you assess learning?
3. Have you led facilitation?

Sample Interview Questions to Ask

Interviews are a two-way street. You have every right to ask as many questions as the interviewee. You need to know what you are getting into and if this is a good fit for you culturally and skill-wise. You also need to make sure that you ask any clarifying questions related to the company and role.

Before the interview, find out who will be in the interview. Sometimes it will be just one person. Other times it might be two or more. Do some research on that person, or if it is a panel, all of them. Be prepared to ask questions related to their work experience and role. LinkedIn is a great place to find the information you need.

1. What would a typical day look like for me?
2. Where do you see the company in five years?
3. How has your role changed since you've been here?
4. What is your favorite part about working here?
5. How will you measure the success of the person in this position?
6. Are there opportunities for growth?
7. What do you see as the most challenging aspect of this job?
8. What characteristics do you look for in employees in order to represent the company's values?
9. What are the greatest qualities of the people who are most successful in this position?
10. Is this a new position or did someone leave?
11. How would you describe the company's culture?
12. How will I know if I'm doing a good job?

Beyond the Bell Bonus Tip:

When you are asked a question, be prepared to answer it and then give an example.

Negotiate

When you get your job offer, be prepared to negotiate. This was a very foreign concept to me because I've never had the opportunity to negotiate anything regarding my job or salary. As teachers, we have a set salary and that's it.

Why should you negotiate?

Negotiating the job offer shows your employer you're confident and understand what you have to offer. It reflects your value and self-worth. The salary you agree upon will impact your future bonuses and promotions with this company because a lot of times they are based upon what you were already making. This will also affect your retirement planning, which could mean a lot of money over the course of your career.

How do you negotiate?

The first step in this process is research. You need to be knowledgeable about the average rate for the position you want. You also need to factor in experience, certifications, and any other qualities that you have that would increase the assets you bring to the company.

Once the company has made the offer, take time to consider everything that has been offered to you. If it is not the right fit, don't be afraid to say no. But if you want the job, negotiate the offer by reminding them of your skills and experience. Express your enthusiasm about working for the company.

What can you negotiate?

Salary is not the only thing you can negotiate. You can also negotiate vacation time, working from home, flexible hours, bonuses, relocation costs, professional development, phone/internet allowance, your title, and start date.

Don't be afraid to negotiate! Ask: You never know what they may be willing to offer.

Online Learning

Coursera
EDX
Udemy
Yukon Learning
LinkedIn Learning
Langevin Learning
Future Learn
ATD
Also look for learning cohorts.
Look for self-paced courses individual people have designed.

Book Recommendations

The Obstacle Is the Way
The Compound Effect
The Design of Everyday Things
Teachers to Trainers
Your Second Life Begins When You Realize You Only Have One
The Proximity Principle
The 2-Hour Job Search
The Proximity Principle
The Alchemist
Chase the Lion
Business Boutique
What Color Is Your Parachute
Atomic Habits
Design for How People Learn
Map It
Design Thinking for Training and Development
E-Learning Department of One
The eLearning Designer's Handbook
The Accidental Instructional Designer

Podcasts

Ken Coleman
Teacher Career Coach
The Jr. High Dropout
Step Away from the Classroom
That's Awesome ID
Share Whatcha Learned
Educators2Educators
Teacher Transitions Podcast
Fabulous Learning Nerds
Accidental Trainer
LxD Talks
Become an IDOL
I'm New Here
Teacher Transition
The Teacher Career Coach
TLDCast

People to Follow on LinkedIn

Cara North
Christy Tucker
Devlin Peck
Jeff Patterson
Nyla Spooner
Ant Pugh
Alexander Salas
Cara North: She posts every day (M–F) a list of L&D jobs.
Laura McNeill
Lisa Spinelli
Nicole Papaioannou Lugara
TPLD group

Resume

Job Scan- https://www.jobscan.co/
Resume Examples: https://bit.ly/3prLEda,
https://bit.ly/353J3fT

Interview Prep on YouTube

Madeline Mann
Andrew LaCivita

Facebook Groups

Bossed Up Courage Community
Get out of Teaching
Life After Teaching
Design for How People Learn
Instructional Designers in Education
ID Career Academy
Freedom Through Remote ID & Elearning
Instructional Design Jobs

YouTube Channels

Devlin Peck
Cara North
Teaching: A Path to L&D
Ant Pugh
Leena Marie Saleh

Where to Look for Job Postings

Glassdoor
Edsurge
Indeed
LinkedIn
ISTE
Outschool
Monster
FlexJobs
ActiveHire
America's Job Exchange
American Education Research Association
Boomerang
Department of Education
Department of Labor
Dice
DiversityJobs
Editorial Freelancers Association
Edweek.org
Highmark
Hired
Idealist
Jopwell
Rehire
TalentZoo

Google for Jobs
LinkUp
USAJobs.gov
Handshake
Ladders
UpWork
AngelList
ZipRecruiter
CareerBuilder
WorkMonger
Job Seek Dashboard

Also reach out to the print and software companies you are familiar with or have used in your school system for career opportunities.

ABOUT THE AUTHOR

Calley loves learning, exploring, and creativity. She has a wide range of hobbies and interests. In her free time, she enjoys being outdoors the most—whether it be hiking with her dog, paddleboarding, or taking pictures. She can be found frequently jet setting around the world and seeking new adventures.

This is her third book. She is also the author of *Revealing Your Masterpiece: Trusting in God's Plan for Your Soulmate* and *Out West In the Mountains.*

Made in the USA
Monee, IL
08 November 2022

17322458R00095